Finally, Porky worked up the courage to ask her out. He had a great day all planned . . .

. . . AND THEN I THOUGHT WE COULD GO TO THE PICTURES, AND FINISH OFF WITH A BACON SARNIE AT MY PLACE. WHAT DO YOU SAY?

That invitation was his first mistake . . .

I BEG YOUR PARDON? DID I HEAR CORRECTLY? GO OUT WITH YOU? YOU MUST BE JOKING, YOU REPULSIVE LITTLE YOKEL! YOU STINK OF PIGS!

No matter which way you look at it, that was no compliment. Porky began to plan his revenge . . .

Now deep in the heart of London lived Porky's cousin Harold. Pigs were the love of his life . . . apart from himself that is . . .

. . . "AND AS A CHIEF EXECUTIVE OF THE PIG IMPROVEMENT BOARD, I STRONGLY RECOMMEND THAT YOU PURCHASE A COPY AS SOON AS POSSIBLE" . . . DID YOU GET ALL THAT, MISS JONES?

Harold (Hal to his friends) was a bit flash. He was often to be seen in a rather nice little motor . . .

. . . And more often with a blonde beside him!

OH HAL, DARLING, IT'S BEEN A WONDERFUL DAY, WHEN CAN I SEE YOU AGAIN?

OH, NOT FOR AT LEAST A MONTH. I'M BOOKED SOLID.

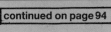
continued on page 94

£2.95

C O N T

2. PHOTO-STORY — Porky's Revenge!

6. STAR MEN! — is he the boy for you?

8. PHOTO-STORY — When Tomorrow Comes

11. PIN-UP — Prince

14. STYLE — Scots Wha-hey!

16. MADONNA FACT FILE

18. THE ART OF PARTIES! — how to throw the perfect party . . .

20. DEAR SANTA, PLEASE BRING ME DANNY KELLY FOR CHRISTMAS . . . — a reader's true experience

22. ARE YOU TALKING TO ME OR CHEWING A BRICK? — I wish I'd said that!

24. BEAUTY + STYLE — 8 pages take you Back To The Future!

32. BE BEASTLY! — Do you purr, growl or bark to get your own way?

36. SWEET FREEDOM — a reader's true experience

39. PHOTO-STORY — Love Can't Turn Around

45. CHOICES . . . — will you, won't you . . .?

46. FEEDBACK SPECIAL! — Test your pop knowledge

◀P8

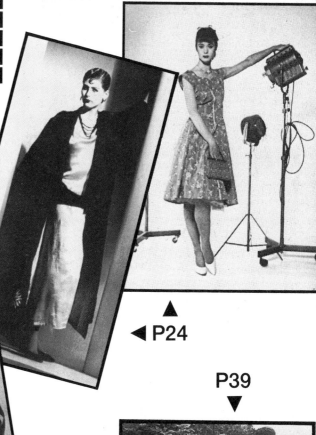

▲
◀ P24

P39
▼

◀P16

E N T S

48. ONLY THE LONELY . . . — How would you cope with loneliness?

50. BEAUTY — All I Wanted Was A Trim . . .!

51. THROUGH THE BARRICADES — a reader's true experience

56. LIGGIN', GIGGIN', AND POSIN'! — The stars are caught by Patches' candid camera

60. WHAT WILL YOU BE DOING IN TEN YEARS TIME? — a careers quiz for you

62. HERE COMES COLLEGE! — all you need to know

64. THE NAME GAME — is yours a guide to your personality?

65. PHOTO-STORY — Ghostbusters!

66. WHAT AN EYE-OPENER! — do you have specs appeal?

71. HORSIN' AROUND — everything you ever wanted to know about horses . . .

74. PICK UP YOUR COAT AND RUN! — the boys to avoid at a party

76. SECOND TIME AROUND! — second hand fashions to make you think again

78. "I WANNA BE IN PICTURES" — a day in the life of a Patches' fashion photographer

80. THAT WAS THEN . . . THIS IS NOW!

81. 'BUT I WANTED TO BE A BRAIN SURGEON . . .' — what do you want to be?

84. PHOTO-STORY — If Your Heart Isn't In It . . .

86. BACKCHAT — tricks to make you look good from behind

90. PIN-UP — Morten Harket

92. BEAT THE BLUES! — feeling a bit down? We'll cheer you up . . .

◀ P78

P84 ▶

◀ P66

P74

The Capricorn Boy.
(Dec. 21 - Jan. 19)

Capricorns can be peculiar, and Capricorn boys more than most. They're argumentative, intolerant, bad-tempered and moody. Still keen? Oh well, no accounting for it! Now you know the worst, you'll be relieved to know they do have one or two good points. This boy is sporty, athletic, and generally quite hunky. He likes parties, and though he's liable to forget dates and forget to call you, he'll never two-time you because he's really quite sweet and faithful. Many Boxer dogs are born under the sign of Capricorn.

This guy will do everything the hard way, but he's clever if not brilliant. There aren't many things the Capricorn guy can't do if he sets his mind to it, including knitting, cooking and typing, so if you're one of these people who likes saying "Men!" with a maternal shake of the head, this guy is not for you.

Although this boy appears outgoing and fun, deep down he's more conservative than Dennis Thatcher, so avoid him if you have radically different views. You have to be thoroughly hooked to go out with a Capricorn, because you'll argue a lot and he'll forget a lot of things. But he's worth hanging on to if you can, 'cos as a rule Capricorns aren't a bad lot.

His ideal girl is one who shares his views, because arguing with him is a lost cause. He also likes you to think he's wonderful, and if you're pretty then so much the better. But don't mess him about, because when a Capricorn falls for someone he falls hard.

Don't ever try to convince this guy he's wrong. There's not a Capricorn alive who'll believe it, let alone admit it.

DAVID BOWIE, JAN 7 — Don't ever try to convince this guy he's wrong.

The Aquarius Boy.
(Jan 20 - Feb 18)

Oh-oh. Dearie me. This guy is — ahem, how can we put it? Let's see. Raving loony seems to sum him up quite nicely. Yes, we'll stick with that. This guy is a raving loony.

Don't get us wrong, though — he's great fun, kind and generous, always thinking up nice surprises for you. While he likes a good argument, he'd do almost anything to avoid falling out with you, and he'll stand up for you if you get hassled. What more could a girl ask for, we hear you cry. But hold your horses. You've overlooked his bad points.

The Aquarian guy is unpredictable, moody and quick-tempered. You'll never understand him without a degree in psychiatry and even then you'd be pushing it. But don't worry too much, because a lot of Aquarians don't want to be understood anyway. They like to be more confusing than anyone else. You'll have to put up with a lot of crazes, and a lot of talk about working in Third World countries, because this guy is a humanitarian and wants to do Good Work. It'll take something drastic for him actually to change his lifestyle to that extent, though, unless he's found his ideal cause.

His ideal girl is someone who will cause heads to turn, who shares his views and will always back him up and encourage him in all his ideas. You'll

have a hectic time if you date an Aquarian. We know a girl who went out with five Aquarian guys one after the other and she was on the brink of a nervous breakdown. But if you split up with an Aquarian boyfriend you'll find he doesn't hold grudges and he'll make a good friend.

Remember, though, that this guy makes the Mad Hatter look like a chartered accountant. Unless you're crazy or a psychoanalyst or both, cross the street when you see him coming.

ALAN ALDA, JAN 28 — He makes the Mad Hatter look like a chartered accountant.

The Pisces Boy
(Feb 19 - Mar 20)

Pisceans are the most misunderstood sign of the Zodiac. The reason for this is that other people find it hard to grasp that when the Piscean calls them "Pigface", "Hound" or "Nellie" (as in the elephant) they are only kidding and mean it in the nicest possible way. Once you have overcome this barrier you'll find your Piscean boy very clever, very funny, very moody and very very romantic. He'll go in the huff for days if you don't come to watch him playing football because he'll think you don't love him any more. He'll buy you roses and hold your hand, but keep a careful eye on him with your friends because he'll ask them extremely personal questions within five minutes of being introduced.

This guy is known far and wide as a Casanova and a ladies' man of the first order. He's a charmer, sure, but a Piscean is very choosy about who he goes out with — and if he's serious he won't mess you about. He does tend

to act like a spoilt six year old quite often, so have a good supply of Smarties on hand to keep him quiet.

His ideal girl is someone who looks good and gets on well with his mum. She must be loyal, loving, and desired by half the male population of the town. Pisceans go for blondes.

You might think there's something rather fishy about your Piscean boy until you know him a bit better. Ignore his reputation and don't worry if he smells a bit funny.

BILL OWEN, MAR 14 — Ignore his reputation, and don't worry if he smells a bit funny.

The Aries Boy
(Mar 21 - Apr 20)

AAARGH! It's an Arian! Handle with care, Danger Explosives and Caution! An Arian only has two moods; good and absolutely awful. When he's in a bad mood the only thing you can do is make it worse, but when he's in a good mood, tread carefully. The last thing you want to do is make him lose his head.

But let's look on the bright side. Arians are generally of a not too bad disposition, and they'll put up with more than their fair share of hassle from their loved ones. If you know how far you can push him, you're on a winner.

Don't think he's all wonderful, though — your typical Arian is extremely obstinate. A mule doesn't have a look in, and he's more pig-neaded than Pinky and Perky put together. Outside of his friends and family, he stands no nonsense from anyone — and Heaven help the poor newsagent who charges him two pence extra on a packet of Chewits!

But if you're in his good books there's nothing he wouldn't do for

 Star

Men!

The Cancer Boy

(June 21 - July 21)

At first glance, he's everything you could ask for. Attractive, popular, witty, amusing, well-dressed, clever — the list seems endless. You could be excused for thinking that this perfect specimen has stepped straight out of your dreams.

Not that we want to shatter your illusions (hee hee) but there are a few things you should know . . .

Don't be taken in by the big blue eyes and innocent look. This boy is a charmer, and he'll charm you out of your new sweater, your favourite album, your money and your mind. Your mum will love him, your sister will fancy him, and your brother will go to the football with him. But beware — the Cancer boy is out for a laugh and a good time, and if he can't have fun with you he won't be long in finding someone more to his taste. There's always a queue of girls waiting for him — you have to bear that in mind.

Another thing to remember is that when you split up with a Cancerian, he's not one of those people who can be "just friends" immediately, and if you give him the elbow, he'll probably bear a grudge for a while.

Their ideal girl is, surprisingly, not a loud, amusing party girl, but the sort of shy, pretty, quiet types everyone likes. Once he's found his ideal girl, he'll be hooked, and he'll even give up his mates for her. Cancerians go for long relationships.

If you fancy this guy first, you have to be a fully-fledged cynic to make a go of a relationship with him, because he'll take complete advantage of you and feel not one scrap of guilt. If he fancies you first, you're on a winner — if you don't mind playing the docile little woman. This guy isn't *quite* a male chauvinist yet — but you can hear him grunting now and again!

you. He's amiable, obliging, but while he's not exactly inconsiderate, he doesn't go out of his way to make life easy for you. But he'll be very upset if you shout at him for it.

His ideal girl is someone who doesn't lose her temper often, and who is prepared to accept his ways without trying to change them. He doesn't worry overmuch about looks, but if you share his sense of humour you're halfway there.

This boy causes scenes in shops. If you can handle that, fine. If, however, you're easily embarrassed and he asks you out, make sure you're otherwise engaged for the next four years.

JULIAN LENNON, APRIL 7 — If you share his sense of humour you're halfway there.

The Taurus Boy

(Apr 21 - May 20)

This boy fancies himself as a bit of a philosopher. He can sort out your problems in the time it takes to make you a hot cup of tea, and to be fair, he's usually able to give you some pretty sound advice. He makes you see things in perspective, and you end up wondering how you could ever have been so silly.

His own personal life, however, is a mess. None of his theories apply to himself, and if the girl he's currently in love with forgets to call he starts contemplating suicide. Taureans make great mates, but lousy boyfriends.

He gets through life doing exactly what he wants. If that ties in with what his teachers or employers want, that's sheer luck. If it doesn't (and it usually doesn't) he can talk his way out of anything. He's intelligent,

creative and dedicated — *if* he's enthusiastic about the project. If he's not, he'll do anything short of committing murder to avoid working. The amount of creativity that goes into inventing excuses would allow him to write a novel a month, and maybe one or two short stories as well.

The demands of the Taurean are modest. His ideal girl is independent, interesting, intelligent and attractive. If you can take a lot of teasing, so much the better, because the Taurean boy is extremely quick-witted and likes making fun of people.

This guy could talk the legs off your labrador then persuade it to go for a walk. On no account lend this man money.

The late PHIL SILVERS, MAY 11 — On no account lend this man money.

The Gemini Boy

(May 21 - June 20)

"I'm not speaking to you ever again! I'm telling my mum what you said!"

What can this be? A five-year-old child falling out with his friend? An infant brother and sister having a little squabble? No no, dear reader, think again — it's a Gemini boy having a tantrum!

Yep, I'm very much afraid that this boy is just a teensy bit huffy. You have to be really careful not to offend him, or he'll be in a big cream puff for days and days — and more often than not you won't have a clue what you've done to upset him. He won't tell you, either — you have to guess.

Once a Gemini guy gets talking, there's nothing you can do to shut him up, save cutting his tongue out with your nail file, and methinks that might be a trifle drastic. You could try telling

him to shut his face, of course, but then you run the risk of him huffing for a week.

On the credit side, many Geminis are very organised people. They're methodical and dedicated — they set their minds on one thing and stick to it. They're great believers in the old saying "if a thing's worth doing, it's worth doing well." Pretty often, Geminis are terminally boring.

Not always, though! They're supposed to be the life and soul of the party — unfortunately only about one in five of them are.

The Gemini boy is often quite musical or artistic — or even both. His ideal girl is someone who's a good listener, and she has to be wildly attractive, but she must only have eyes for him.

This boy is quite content to look like Worzel Gummidge, but his aftershave could stun an elephant at ten paces. A clothes peg is essential if you intend this to be a long relationship.

JOHN TAYLOR, JUNE 20 — His aftershave could stun an elephant at ten paces.

GEORGE MICHAEL, JUNE 25 — Once he's found his ideal girl, he's hooked.

I'm pretty close to my kid sister, Jenny. We write a lot when I'm away at sea . . .

HI, FOLKS! HOME IS THE SAILOR, HOME FROM THE SEA! WELL, FOR THREE WEEKS ANYWAY!

HELLO, BOB. YOU'RE LOOKING WELL . . .

When Tomorrow Comes

YOU HAVEN'T ASKED ME WHAT I'VE BROUGHT FOR YOU THIS TIME, JENNY. USUALLY YOU'RE DYING TO KNOW.

I ALREADY KNOW, DON'T I? YOU ALWAYS BRING ME THE SAME THING WHEN YOU COME HOME ON LEAVE.

ANOTHER DOLL. IT'S BEAUTIFUL, BOB. I'VE NEVER SEEN ONE LIKE IT BEFORE.

IT'S VERY RARE. ALMOST ONE OF A KIND. I PICKED IT UP IN GREECE.

Jenny had been a collector for years . . .

I SOMETIMES WONDER IF I'M GETTING TOO OLD TO COLLECT DOLLS. I STILL ENJOY IT, THOUGH . . .

THAT'S ALL THAT MATTERS, THEN.

WELL, ACTUALLY, THERE IS SOMETHING ELSE THAT MATTERS TO ME AS WELL NOWADAYS . . .

And next day . . .

THIS IS KEITH, MY BOYFRIEND. KEITH, I'D LIKE YOU TO MEET MY FABULOUS BIG BROTHER, BOB.

HI, PLEASED TO MEET YOU. JENNY TALKS ABOUT YOU ALL THE TIME.

SHE SEEMS REALLY BRIGHT AND EXCITED, MUM. IS SHE SERIOUS ABOUT THIS GUY?

VERY SERIOUS! AS FAR AS JENNY'S CONCERNED SHE'S HEAD-OVER-HEELS IN LOVE!

I GUESS I DIDN'T REALISE, I HAVEN'T BEEN AROUND TO SEE IT, BUT MY LITTLE SISTER IS REALLY GROWING UP!

And she couldn't have been happier . . .

WHAT D'YOU WANT TO DO, THEN?

I DON'T CARE, AS LONG AS I'M WITH YOU. I JUST WISH WE COULD BE TOGETHER EVERY SINGLE MINUTE, KEITH!

But of course, they couldn't be . . .

I'M NOT SEEING KEITH TONIGHT. HE'S GOT A PART-TIME JOB A COUPLE OF EVENINGS A WEEK. BRENDA'S COMING OVER INSTEAD . . .

YOU TWO HAVE BEEN BEST FRIENDS SINCE YOU WERE IN NAPPIES. DON'T YOU EVER GET SICK OF EACH OTHER?

WELL, IF YOU'RE GOING TO PLAY RECORDS ALL NIGHT, I'LL HAVE TO GO OUT FOR SOME PEACE. I'M GOING TO SEE A FEW FRIENDS.

But on the way . . .

KEITH. WITH ANOTHER GIRL! AND THEY CLEARLY KNOW EACH OTHER PRETTY WELL. IS HE TWO-TIMING JENNY?

IT'S NONE OF MY BUSINESS, I KNOW. BUT IF JENNY SOMEHOW FINDS OUT ABOUT THIS, SHE'LL BE REALLY BADLY HURT . . .

'Cos she was crazy about the guy . . .

I'VE NEVER FELT ANYTHING LIKE IT BEFORE, BOB. I LOVE HIM SO MUCH. AND HE LOVES ME.

SHE TALKS ABOUT HIM ALL THE TIME. IT'S OBVIOUS THAT SHE THINKS SHE'S THE ONLY GIRL HE'S SEEING.

And that's what he wanted her to believe . . .

HI, JEN! I'VE MISSED YOU. I HATE IT WHEN WE DON'T SEE EACH OTHER.

ME, TOO! BUT WE CAN MAKE UP FOR IT THIS EVENING!

WHENEVER SHE'S NOT OUT WITH KEITH, SHE SEES BRENDA . . .

Continued on page 12

Star Men!

(continued from p.7)

The Leo Boy
(July 22 - Aug 21)

Is it a bird? Is it Martin Degville? Nope — it's a real live honest to goodness Leo!

He's wild, outrageous, the sort of guy people stare at in the street — seven foot hair in varying colours and skin tight leather trousers. But don't be misled by the way he looks — the Leo boy is very clever indeed as a rule, and he has the potential to be really bright. He's probably passed about twenty four 'O' levels, but if he's at college or University you'll find he's a bit of a waster. He'll cry on your shoulder about failed tests and exams and promise faithfully to do more work and less partying. And you'll believe him, because he really does mean it — but then a friend phones and asks him to come out, and his good intentions are shelved until the next failed exam.

While he wouldn't two-time you — well, not as such — well, only now and again — he doesn't go out looking for girls, but if one comes along and you're not around, he might find it hard to say no. Leos find it very hard to resist temptation, on account of having no willpower whatsoever. Leos don't make very good priests.

If you like being seen in the company of a friendly Yeti, this is the guy for you. If you're the jealous type, however, give the Leo boy a miss, because he's so friendly and likeable that he goes out of his way to speak to all his mates when you're out — and you can bet your last Jelly Tot that half of them will be girls.

The Leo guy is full of wild and ambitious plans about going abroad to live and work, but they'll never amount to anything because he's permanently skint. If you've heard the expression "a fool and his money are soon parted", you'll be interested to know that the original fool is commonly believed to have been a Leo.

His ideal girl is someone with a fun sense of humour. He goes for all different types, and looks aren't very important to him. You'll have to be able to converse fluently about the Gun Club, Crass and the Plasmatics. If you're a closet Tom Jones fan, hide in there with him until this guy has gone.

PETE BURNS, AUG 5 — Don't be misled by the way he looks.

The Virgo Boy
(Aug 22 - Sept 21)

You'll have no problems making friends with the Virgo boy — he likes to have lots of people round him, and he finds it really easy to make friends. Girls like him — boys don't, because if the truth be told, he *is* a little bit of a plonker. Because he's a genuinely nice guy, and as a rule quite good-looking, girls can overlook this, but boys just find him annoying.

Virgo boys usually have something about them that makes them a little bit special — incredible looks, a lifestyle that's a bit different — anything to take away from the fact that basically they're very ordinary people and none too bright either.

Unfortunately, you have to watch this guy like a hawk. He's a real flirt, and as soon as a new girl comes on the scene, his eyes'll light up, and he'll be over there like a striking snake, leaving you fuming into your Diet Pepsi. You have to learn not to take it too seriously if he makes off with a new girl every month or two. More than likely he'll come back to you, but if you don't think you can handle it, don't get involved in the first place.

As far as work goes, he expects everything on a plate without having to do a stroke. He can and will work extremely hard, but he grudges every minute of it.

His ideal girl is stunning — but brains aren't important. Just make sure you're thick enough to think he's wonderful, or bright enough to pretend you do. Sure, he's a bit of a playboy, but he doesn't try to hurt anyone. He manages perfectly well unintentionally.

A Virgo boy is your typical male. You're expected to be his girlfriend, sister and mother all rolled into one — it's also very handy if you're a qualified nursery nurse. He's cute and sweet and loving. Don't trust him an inch.

MICHAEL JACKSON, AUG 29 — Girls like him, boys don't.

The Libra Boy
(Sept 22 - Oct 22)

This one could cause you a few problems. You'd better get that straight from the start. Unless you're just like him, you'll never understand him, so if you're not prepared to try hard, give him a swerve.

The Libra boy has no illusions about himself. He knows he's lazy, he's aware he'll let you do everything for him, and he doesn't deny that he's untidy. But like most guys, he thinks that as long as he admits to his faults, that makes everything OK. It won't occur to him to try to change!

Many Librans are good at sport — so check that out well before you get involved with a football maniac and have to spend every Saturday watching him play! Sport or another interest will probably be your only rival, though, 'cos the Libra guy won't two time you — he knows when he's well off!

Quite often he's musical — but he puts himself down, and he keeps his feelings well hidden — but don't make the mistake of thinking he doesn't care.

His ideal girl is someone who's quite happy to do all the work for him, but is still an individual in her own right. You should be able to talk about his interests or he'll feel obliged to educate you.

Make sure you know what you're letting yourself in for before you go out with a Libra boy. They're very strange.

JULAN COPE, OCT 21 — He's very strange.

The Scorpio Boy
(Oct 23 - Nov 21)

A little bit silly, this one. The Scorpio boy tends to be a bit childish, so if you're easily irritated, steer well clear. Whatever the project they're involved with, you'll find that Scorpio boys will throw themselves into it wholeheartedly. In fact, they'll think, talk, dream, sleep and eat whatever it is they're currently involved with, and if you don't share his enthusiasm, you might find yourself getting just a teensy bit bored.

On the credit side, though, you'll find him pleasant and friendly, well-mannered and often quite artistic. Your friends will love him, and more than likely they won't be able to understand why you keep moaning about him — but they don't have to put up with his undying enthusiasm for everything except you!

The Scorpio guy is keen to do

things well. He learns new skills quickly, and he's very adaptable. This means that although he's more than capable of helping you do your mum's shopping and making the beds, his creative streak supplies him with plenty of excuses.

His ideal girl is someone who shares his interests and wild enthusiasm. If you're not the enthusiastic sort, make sure you're a good actress, or he might lose patience with your lack of interest.

Unless you're the school marm type, you'll find this guy a little hard to manage. Buy yourself a metre stick and crack him round the head at regular intervals.

MAGS, NOV 1 — If you're easily irritated, steer well clear.

The Sagittarius Boy
(Nov 22 - Dec 20)

The Sagittarius guy is keen to do well. He's determined. He sets his eye on his goal and goes for it, which is great if it's you he's after, but not so great if it's your best friend.

Unfortunately, the Sagittarius boy is concerned with himself and his own ambitions, first and foremost. You might be important to him, but don't ever make the mistake of thinking that you're more important than he is.

A lot of girls are fooled by the Sagittarian's looks. Sure, he appears to be a rebel who doesn't care about anything, but in reality he cares very much about what he wants to do. He's not afraid of hard work if it means the results he's after in the long run.

His ideal girl is an exceptional sort of person. She's an amateur psychiatrist, and she has her own interests and friends — but she's always on hand when he needs her. Telepathy and an unlimited bus pass are essential for the Sagittarian's girl.

This guy does have some good points, though. He's very friendly and likeable, and if he sets out to do something he gets it done. He's reliable — he won't leave you standing outside the ABC in the snow for half an hour. Don't worry about this guy two timing you — if he wants to finish it, he'll tell you straight.

If you're the type of girl who calls people swot and toady, avoid this guy at all costs, because his passion for hard work will drive you crazy. Get yourself another boyfriend for the nights he's working.

BILLY IDOL, NOV 30 — He's concerned with himself, first and foremost.

... WHICH LEAVES KEITH FREE TO SEE OTHER GIRLS. AND BY THE LOOK OF IT, HE HAS PLENTY TO CHOOSE FROM.

BUT HOW CAN I TELL JENNY THAT? HAVE I GOT THE RIGHT TO — BREAK HER HEART?

THAT'S OK, BRENDA. IF I CAN'T SEE YOU TONIGHT I'LL JUST STAY IN AND WASH MY HAIR OR SOMETHING.

HEY, IF YOU'RE NOT SEEING KEITH, AND BRENDA'S STOOD YOU UP, WHY DON'T YOU LET ME TAKE YOU TO THE PICTURES?

TERRIFIC! THAT'S A GREAT IDEA!

But it wasn't such a good idea after all . . .

KEITH? I THOUGHT YOU WERE WORKING TONIGHT. AND BRENDA! WH-WHAT'S GOING ON?

OH, HECK, JENNY. I CAN EXPLAIN . . .

WHAT IS THERE TO EXPLAIN? JUST 'COS I'M SEEING YOU DOESN'T MEAN I CAN'T SEE OTHER GIRLS AS WELL, JENNY.

BUT I THOUGHT I WAS THE ONLY ONE . . . YOU SAID I WAS. YOU TOLD ME I WAS SPECIAL.

SURE, 'COS THAT'S WHAT YOU WANTED TO HEAR. C'MON, JEN, DON'T BE A KID ABOUT THIS, OR YOU MIGHT AS WELL RUN HOME TO YOUR DOLLY COLLECTION RIGHT NOW . . .

Jenny ran off in tears . . .

JENNY, WAIT!

YOU'RE THE ONE WHO SHOULD GROW UP, SON! YOU CAN'T TREAT PEOPLE LIKE THEY WERE DOLLS, Y'KNOW, WITH NO FEELINGS . . .

AND YOU'RE MEANT TO BE JENNY'S FRIEND, BRENDA! YOU'RE SUPPOSED TO CARE ABOUT HER!

I DO! I'M SORRY, BOB. HONEST. SHE WASN'T MEANT TO FIND OUT LIKE THIS . . .

But I wasn't listening. I wanted to get home to find Jenny...

JENNY, WHAT'S HAPPENED TO YOUR DOLLS? I WENT TO LOOK FOR YOU IN YOUR ROOM AND I SAW THEM ALL BROKEN...

I DID IT ON PURPOSE! I'M FINISHED WITH ALL THAT KIDS' STUFF! I'M NEVER GOING TO COLLECT ANYTHING AGAIN!

THAT'S JUST WHAT KEITH'S BEEN DOING, ISN'T IT? COLLECTING DOLLS! I BET BRENDA WASN'T THE ONLY ONE. HE'S MADE A COMPLETE FOOL OF ME!

WELL, I NEVER WANT ANYTHING TO DO WITH HIM AGAIN! OR WITH ANY OTHER GUY! I'M FINISHED WITH LOVE!

NO, YOU HAVEN'T. YOU'VE JUST STARTED. YOU FEEL HURT AND BETRAYED RIGHT NOW, JENNY. BUT YOU'LL GET OVER IT.

IT HAPPENS TO ALMOST EVERYONE, JENNY. FALLING IN LOVE, GETTING HURT, GETTING OVER IT. IT'S PART OF GROWING UP.

I MET A GIRL IN GERMANY, YOU KNOW. I ADORED HER, AND THOUGHT SHE FELT THE SAME. BUT IT TURNED OUT SHE HAD ANOTHER GUY...

IT'S FUNNY. I NEVER THOUGHT ABOUT YOU FALLING IN LOVE. YOU'VE ALWAYS JUST BEEN MY STRONG, BRAVE, BIG BROTHER.

AND YOU'VE ALWAYS JUST BEEN MY KID SISTER! BUT WE'RE GROWN UP NOW, JENNY. I GOT OVER MY BROKEN HEART. YOU'LL GET OVER YOURS.

WAS THAT STORY TRUE? YOU DIDN'T THINK IT UP JUST TO MAKE ME FEEL BETTER?

HEY, I'M YOUR BIG BROTHER. TRUST ME! ONE DAY YOU'LL GET OVER KEITH. ONE DAY YOU MIGHT EVEN FORGIVE BRENDA...

"One day you'll meet someone new. Someone you'll want to share every minute with again..."

"And that's when you'll know..."

I WROTE TO MY BROTHER LAST WEEK, TO TELL HIM ABOUT YOU. HE SENT ME THIS...

WHAT IS IT?

A DOLL? IT'S PRETTY.

IT'S MORE THAN THAT. IT'S A MESSAGE — HIS WAY OF TELLING ME HE WAS RIGHT ABOUT ME GETTING OVER MY BROKEN HEART.

IT'S HIS WAY OF TELLING ME IT'S TIME TO START AGAIN. IN MORE WAYS THAN ONE.

THE END

13

"I DON'T CARE IF YOU'VE SEEN LORNA DOONE THERE, I'M NOT LOOKING DOWN!"

ALL OUR CLOTHES WERE GATHERED FROM JUMBLE SALES AND CHARITY SHOPS — PRICES RANGING FROM 30p-£4. ALL JEWELLERY FROM A SELECTION BY JOE COOL.

OUR THANKS TO THE STAFF OF BORTHWICK CASTLE, NR. EDINBURGH.

S·C·O·T·S
Wha-hey!

SEARCH THROUGH THE JUMBLE SALES AND CHARITY SHOPS FOR TARTAN, PLAID AND TWEED TO CREATE YOUR OWN SCOTTISH STYLE. AFTER ALL, THERE'S MORE TO THE HIGHLANDS THAN HEATHER, HAMISHES AND HAGGIS.

ONE WAY OF WARMING UP BEFORE
YOUR PORRIDGE — A QUICK BIT OF
HIGHLAND DANCING.

STAND OUT LOUDLY FROM THE CROWD
BY MIXING TARTANS TOGETHER — IF THAT
DOESN'T WORK, INVEST IN A SET OF
BAGPIPES.

GET ON THE RIGHT TRACK IN WARM
WOOLLEN TROUSERS — ADD A BROAD
BELT AND BRACES IF THEY'RE TOO LONG.

TAKE TO THE SUNSHINE IN REFLECTIVE
MOOD WITH CREAMY COTTON OVER
MUTED TARTAN SKIRTS.

MADONNA

FACT FILE

NAME: Madonna Louise Penn.
PLACE OF BIRTH: Michigan.
DATE OF BIRTH: 16th August, 1959.
STARSIGN: Leo.
EDUCATION: Won a scholarship to study dance at the University of Michigan.
COLOUR OF HAIR: Naturally dark brown.
FAVOURITE FILM: "Gentlemen Prefer Blondes".
FAVOURITE COLOUR: Turquoise.
FAVOURITE FOOD: "Popcorn — my favourite food in the world. It cleans your system, it fills you up, and it's cheap!"
FAVOURITE DRINK: Campari and grapefruit juice.
FIRST RECORD BOUGHT: Either *Incense and Peppermints* by The Strawberry Alarm Clock or *The Letter* by The Box Tops.
PREVIOUS JOBS: Working in various fast-food restaurants such as "Dunkin' Donuts" in New York; she later did some nude modelling — "You got paid ten dollars an hour versus a dollar fifty at *Burger King*," she says.
EXERCISE ROUTINE: Jogging every day, dance exercises, swimming — "I wasn't born with a perfect body. There's a lot of dieting and exercise to me."
CHILDHOOD INFLUENCES: "I watched television a lot and I used to copy Shirley Temple . . . I used to turn on the record player and dance in the basement by myself and give dance lessons to my girlfriends in my five-year-old manner."
IF SHE COULD CHANGE ONE THING ABOUT HER APPEARANCE . . .? "I wish I was taller. I probably look taller because I have a big mouth." (She's 5 ft. 4 ins.)
MOST FRIGHTENING MOMENT: The night the electric fire in her flat set the carpet on fire. "I jumped up and dumped water on it, which made it spread more. Then, my night gown caught fire. I took it off, got dressed, grabbed a few things like my underpants and stuff — and ran for it!"
FIRST LOVE: Ronny Howard from the Fifth Grade at school — "He was beautiful. I wrote my name all over his sneakers and on the playground. I used to take off the top part of my uniform and chase him around."
FAVOURITE TYPE OF GUY: "I prefer effeminate-looking men and young boys. There are lots of very sweet Puerto Rican boys where I live . . . fifteen or sixteen year old boys are the best, and I like smooth, thin men who aren't afraid to show their emotions and cry."

THE ART OF PARTIES

But — there's the other side of the party scene, too. Remember last year when someone was sick behind the sofa? Remember that girl who was howling on a pile of coats in the bedroom? Remember what someone said about that boy you fancied, and how it all turned out to be a pack of lies, but by then it was too late for you to try to get him back?

So this year's your chance to start out all over again in a sparkling mood, by learning from last year's mistakes, or coping with this year's problems before they arise!

PARTY DOLLS

First of all, there's the problem of what to wear to a party. Everyone's chatting about new clothes and new hairstyles, and you're feeling more and more insecure, because you haven't got enough money to splash out on an outfit, and when they ask, "What're *you* wearing?", you just say "Um . . ." and think about the blue skirt with the tomato ketchup stain down the front, or the tight trousers you can no longer get into. But don't panic! Most parties are so packed, and so dimly-lit, that no-one would notice if you went in your kid brother's Superman pyjamas!

Concentrate on your head and neck, the bits that people will notice. Splash out your pocket money on glittery bits for your hair. Wear exotic earrings. Put gold dust on your cheeks and shoulders, and be bold with eyeshadows and lipsticks. And most important of all — remember to smile. It won't matter what you're wearing so long as you look like you're having fun!

DRINKING

All parties should have an endless supply of refreshments — after all dancing's a thirsty business — but this doesn't necessarily

mean alcohol. In fact, alcohol often puts a damper on festivities.

If you're not used to it, it can affect you in many strange ways. After one drink you may feel less self-conscious, and more able to join in the party spirit. But it's hard to know when you've had enough until it's too late and you end up doing a fan-dance on the dining-room table and falling asleep in front of the Christmas tree.

That's why you'd be better off making yourself a huge interesting-looking cocktail of fruit juices and mineral water, and topping it with an umbrella and a cherry. It'll make you stand out in a crowd, and you'll be able to

stand up all evening. And the next morning, you'll still remember every magical moment!

PARTY TEARS

Unfortunately, while parties provide the best opportunities for romance, they also provide the best opportunities for a bust-up. Your boyfriend kisses someone under the mistletoe for just a split second longer than is strictly necessary, and you see your world falling down around your ears. Or he takes the opportunity, while you're dancing just a little too closely with another boy, to tell you that you're welcome to

spend the rest of your life with the wally!

It's because there are so many interesting-looking people and interesting chances at parties that couples decide they're finally bored with each other and it's time to move on. And that's why there's always someone crying in the kitchen at a party. Her boyfriend just struck up a new friendship, and she's been left in the lurch.

If that happens to you, don't waste your time drying your tears on a limp lettuce leaf. There are always other people at parties who end up hanging around feeling a bit left out, so chat to them, make their day and forget your own troubles at the same time!

18

It's party time again! Time to rake out last year's favourite outfit and give it a new lease of life. Time to experiment with daring make-up and use a whole can of mousse on your hair. Time for romance as your hand and his reach out for the last pickled onion at exactly the same moment. Time for soft lights and loud music and cuddles on the stairs.

PARTY BINGEING

Or perhaps you're one of those girls who arrives at a party, feels instantly alone, and races into the kitchen for first grabs at the sausage rolls. If you're the sort who can't cope very well with crowds, and who gorges on a block of chocolate every time she feels threatened, then a party is a great excuse for a pig-out, and by the end of the party season, you're a stone heavier, and not a lot happier.

First of all, try to work out *why* you eat for comfort. Is it that something in your hands stops them shaking, and that something in your mouth gives you a good excuse not to talk?

Or is it just that fatty foods and sugar give you an instant lift, and make you feel able to get through the evening?

If it's the second reason, you're probably well on the way to sorting out your bingeing problem, because you only use it to get yourself going. If it's the first reason, then you've got to try to sort out your mouth/hand problems before everyone starts thinking of you as Miss Piggy. To settle your shaking hands, why not carry a plate of sausage rolls round the crowd? You can meet a lot of interesting people that way! To settle your "What on earth do I say?" problem, try smiling instead, or grab a party hooter, and appear to be

joining in the fun.

But don't lurk in the kitchen, scoffing everything in sight. It's no substitute for the real comfort you can find in becoming part of the party!

CONVERSATION

Shy girls can get far too worked up at the prospect of having to face conversation, too. If you're nervous about parties, you can spend hours practising party chatter in front of your bedroom mirror, before deciding, at the very last minute, that you just can't go through with the hassle, and you end up staying in to wash your hair instead.

Relax! The great thing about parties is that they're noisy. No-one expects you to rabbit on about the quadraphonic sound or tell your life story. A smile's enough to start with. And by the time someone's grabbed you to dance, brought you another Coke, and asked you what you think of the music, you'll feel you've known him for months and be quite happy to walk home with him, laughing about how well the party went.

Party conversation is easy when you know how. So, if you're a bit wary about meeting new people, get out into a noisy Christmas crowd!

Have a great time!

Dear Santa,

Please bring me Danny Kelly for Christmas...

Saturday 13th December

Tore up my Christmas List and re-wrote it. Headed it, 'Danny Kelly'. Didn't think it worth giving to Mum as she'd have a tough time trying to find a copy in Boots.

Considered stuffing list up chimney in the hope that S. Claus might work the old magic but lacked faith — and chimney. Lay on bed for whole of morning dreaming of Danny Kelly's blue eyes and wondering why he's come back to our neighbourhood after all this time . . .

"Have you died up there?" Mum's voice.

I recalled stack of dirty dishes in sink and took stairs at a brisk trot, falling over cat lying in usual fat heap half-way up.

"I've been writing my Christmas cards," I lied. "By the way, d'you think Dad will let me do a paper-round?"

"You? Work?" She made it sound like I'd suggested becoming a mud wrestler. "What brought this on?"

"Would you believe, money? It being nearly Christmas and all of you expecting presents. The miserable pittance Dad doles out won't run to more than a couple of gift-tags."

"Ah," said Mum, eyeing me thoughtfully in her famous "there-is-more-to-this-than-I-can-put-my-finger-on" fashion. I don't know why she bothers typing letters for Simpson, Lloyd and Little; she could be Head of Scotland Yard in no time flat with her detective talents. "I'm surprised you haven't put in for a rise in pocket money."

"I did. Last week. He said he'd see."

"See you clean your room, iron the odd shirt or even sweep a few leaves from the drive, perhaps?"

"Honestly! It's worse than the salt mines round here," I grumbled, shooting out the back door.

I called in at my friend Becky's house to tell her about seeing Danny Kelly in the paper shop but she'd gone out shopping with her mum. If she's gone to the supermarket she's a big creep and I'll tell her so.

Sunday 14th December

Spent the evening at Becky's house trying on all the super new gear her mum's bought her for Christmas.

"No point waiting till Christmas morning when you're not a kid," she said, posing about in purple leggings. "What d'you reckon? Spot on with my silver top for the End-of-Term disco?"

"Fantastic." I was greener than my eye-shadow.

"What are you getting anyway?" she asked, crashing down on the bed beside me.

"Oh, zillions of things if I'm lucky. I began the list last July. But wait till I tell you what I really fancy in my little woolly sock . . ."

So I gave her the picture. Me, romping all unawares into the shop and him, Danny, that is, sort of draped against the newspaper stand with an empty sack at his feet. It was his eyes I remembered, blue as a Siamese cat's, with spiky black lashes growing thickly all round.

Last time I'd seen those eyes they'd been staring out of the dirty, tear-streaked face of an eight-year-old kid who was never out of trouble and whose family were known as the Fighting Kellys. I wasn't supposed to even speak to any of the Kelly brothers even though Danny was in our class at school. My Mum thought they were the pits.

Now the face was clean and the tangled, dusty-coloured hair was glossy and well-cut. He stuck his hands in the pockets of his faded, immaculate jeans and I noticed his jacket was black leather . . .

"I know you," I blurted out, before I could stop myself. "You're Danny Kelly. We were at Yew Tree Primary . . ."

"Suzanne Davidson," he drawled. Very smooth — with that faint lilt that must have been Irish though I never knew the Kellys to go anywhere further than the end of the bus-route. "Clever little Suzi with the big red apple for her lunch every day."

I went all hot. Flashback of me on a windy day in the playground, all togged up in my warm duffel coat and pull-on hat, and dirty Danny Kelly shivering in his washed-out sweatshirt, pausing in his game of football to gaze at my break-time apple.

"Well," I muttered, stuck for a reply. "Long time, huh? I'll take these cards, Mr Dickson, please."

"There's your change, Suzi. Don't you take my new paper lad's mind off his work now, will you. I'm short-handed enough."

I shot one more look at Danny before I left. He smiled, a lovely, gentle smile that I remembered used to get him out of

bother oh, so many times; only now it made me just think of his mouth and what it might feel like if he kissed me.

Becky said, "D . . . D . . . Danny? That kid with the stammer who used to chew his reading card to bits and his brothers skived off school all the time? I don't believe it. You mean he's grown into something tasty?"

I nodded. "Just you wait and see."

Monday 15th December

Set my alarm for something around dawn so I'd be sure to catch Danny delivering our morning news rag. Heard scrunching sound of van tyres and shot out of front door in time to collide heavily with milkman carrying eggs. Instant omelette.

"Sorry," I gasped, fielding a carton of yoghurt and hopping from one bare foot to the other on the icy step.

I stood there, all poised with my freshly-brushed smile and three layers of mascara only, a second before impact, I dropped one of the milk bottles and smashed it to bits.

"Get inside, you silly girl. You've nothing on your feet!" screamed Mum, appearing suddenly like one of those demons in a pantomime who spring out of trap doors in a green flash. She hawked me away from the glass and mess before Danny could get so much as a glimpse of me in my "I've been on the Radio One Road Show" T-shirt which I wear as a nightie.

Will I ever get my act together I wonder?

Tuesday 16th December

Becky has been converted.

"Hey, I saw him. D . . . D . . . Danny boy. He was in the paper shop when I went in. Talk about frogs turning into handsome princes! Who kissed him, I wonder?"

"I know who'd like to," I muttered under my breath.

"Have you found out any more about why he's come back though?" cut in

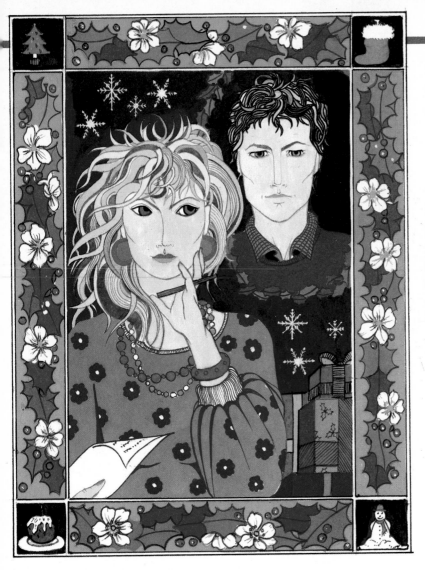

"Slight food-poisoning," he mumbled, after poking me about in embarrassing places with his sausage-pink fingers. "Keep her on liquids for a couple of days. Warmth and quiet. That should do it."

"Will I be O.K. by Saturday?" I whispered. Did he realise it was the End-of-Term disco or was the man completely out of touch?

"Probably. Better to stay indoors, though, until you're fully fit."

I closed my eyes and sank back into the pillows. There was no way I was staying in on Saturday night. I'd be at that disco if I had to dance round my plastic bucket!

Saturday 20th December

Tottered out of bed and straight onto the bathroom scales. A whole five pounds thinner! I'd be able to wear my silver-grey leggings without looking like Nelly the Elephant. Forced down the pieces of toast under Mum's eagle gaze and offered to clean Dad's car as proof of full return to bouncing health.

I was halfway through soaping the bonnet when Becky arrived.

"Enter Miss Marple," she grinned, leaping over the hose-pipe. "I've been busy sleuthing for you while you've been lazing about in your pit."

"The story is," she said, perching herself happily on my old bike, "that, after they'd all been in care for a bit, Danny got himself fostered by a family who lived Monkton way and the two older ones eventually joined the army or the Marines or something.

"Anyway, the foster father's now got a job with the Council and they've moved to Rowland Avenue. So it seems like Danny will be coming to our place in January. How about that then?"

"Brilliant. I'm impressed."

"Brownie points for research, eh? Actually, Mr Dickson told me where he lived when I was pretending to admire the hideous robins on his wrapping paper."

And hanging about waiting for Danny to show up, I thought. I just knew that if she'd gone to a lot of trouble to ferret out information it wasn't for my benefit. Definitely not.

The way she looked that evening she could have been expecting A-ha to show up. The hair, the make-up, the clothes — everything was just amazing and it was my painful duty to tell her so.

"You're looking pretty knock-out yourself," she replied, taking in the slimness and the sexy (I hoped) satin shirt I was wearing.

Pulling was no problem for either of us — probably because we weren't interested. Except in one person.

I caught Becky glancing at her watch as the night wore on. "Expecting somebody?" I said, casually, of course.

"No," she shrugged, but she looked beyond my left ear as she spoke and she never looks at you properly when she's lying. Then her expression changed and **continued on page 34**

Becky, betraying an interest that did nothing to improve a rotten start to the day. "Where's he living? Is he coming to our dump? I mean, if he's got a paper round job he must be planning on staying around."

"I worked that out myself," I replied coldly. Who did she think she was — the CIA? "I also know that when he left the Primary they were all put into care because they didn't have a mother, did they? She died I think. And their dad got put away. Steve told me that."

"Really?" Becky's eyes widened. "I wonder what for. I bet it was GBH. He was always belting those lads. He was violent, you know." When she said "violent" her mouth went all prim.

"Was he?" I shrugged. "It's all ages ago now. You sound like my mum. 'I hope you won't be mixing with that Kelly boy now he's back' she said. She's such a snob!"

"Well, I'm not!" snapped Becky. "And if you want to know something really interesting, he wasn't on his own when I saw him. He had a girl with him, a very pretty blonde girl she was, and, in case it's escaped your memory, I should remind you — Danny Kelly didn't have a sister."

It doesn't do to criticise Becky. She has a very short fuse.

Wednesday 17th December

Had a disgusting Christmas dinner at school. One centimetre of turkey and a pile of soggy sprouts followed by burnt pudding and a sauce you could have used to paste wallpaper on with. Felt distinctly ill all afternoon and barely managed to limp home before collapsing into bed.

"Just a tummy-bug," announced Mum, fussing about with barley-water (and a bucket just in case).

"You should report that canteen to the Public Health," I groaned. "It's salmonella paradise."

"Nonsense. A twenty-four hour virus at the most. You'll be fine by tomorrow."

I swear if I were lying smashed to pieces under a bus she'd say, "Just a twenty-four hour virus. You'll be fine by tomorrow."

Thursday 18th December

I was not fine. I was a lot worse. She had to send for the doctor which was jolly satisfying even if I was burning up with fever and racked with pain.

21

"Are you talking to

It's happened to all of us. You find yourself in a really awkward, embarrassing or downright awful situation, and you can't think of a thing to say! So you bluff your way out of it, and end up making everything worse.
But fear not, gentle reader! Patches comes to your rescue yet again! Read on, and you'll see what you *should* have said to make the best of the situation!

You thought it was safe. You thought you would come through it unscathed. How could your boyfriend ever find out if you went out on a sly date with Andy, your school's answer to Tom Cruise?

But it is not to be. There you are, the two of you, wandering home arm in arm, gazing lovingly into each other's fish suppers, when who should you spot stumping up the road but boring Billy, your boyfriend.

Admittedly this is a tricky situation. In a split second you will have to face a thousand temptations — run, pretend you don't know him, cry, kill yourself — but all of these are dead giveaways (especially the last one) and must be avoided at all costs.

WHAT YOU SHOULD SAY:
"Billy! Hi, how're you doing? You know Andy, don't you? Well, he's mad about Carol, you know, my best mate, and we've just been working out how he should ask her out. He's going to phone her as soon as he gets in!"

WHAT YOU WILL SAY: *"It's Billy! Oh my God, Andy, it's Billy! What am I going to do? Look, Andy, you're my cousin, right? Right? Oh God, I knew I shouldn't have started this. Oh — hi, Billy, what a surprise. This is my cousin Andy. Isn't it Andy? I bet you never knew we were cousins, did you? Well we are! Honest!"*

Well, it's happened again. It always

happens to you, doesn't it? You're holding on to your best mate's fag while she nips into the corner shop for her lunch when who do you see advancing down the hill like Darth Vader? Morten Harket? Robbie Coltrane? Nope — it's your maths teacher.

Now teachers vary. There are the OK sorts, the horrible sorts and the quite-nice-in-fact-almost-human sorts. But whatever type he is, it is unlikely he will ignore the fact that you have a cigarette in your hand.

WHAT YOU SHOULD SAY:
"Well, Sir, as a matter of fact I'm sixteen, and I can have a fag if I feel like it. But actually I'm holding on to this for Big Brenda — you know, the one who's just out of Borstal . . . "

WHAT YOU DO SAY: *"Yeeek! Oh, hello, sir! What? There's nothing behind my back, sir!*
"Oh — where did that come from? It's not mine, sir, honestly! No, really, I haven't a clue how that got there."

You've just wriggled into your superextramegatight jeans and applied an extra three coats of mascara when the phone rings. "Hallo, luv," your boyfriend says casually. "Just thought I'd let you know that I'm having a night out with the lads tonight. I'll see you tomorrow, then."

Now to be fair, he hadn't said he was coming up tonight, and it *was* nice of him to call. But you're disappointed and at the same time you don't want him to know that you're miffed. He's entitled to his nights out with the lads after all, and you don't want him to think you're too possessive.

WHAT YOU SHOULD SAY:
"That's perfectly OK, Bill! As a matter of fact I was just going to give Carol a call — her cousin's staying with her, and she wants me to keep him company while she goes out with Andy . . . "

WHAT YOU DO SAY: *"No, no, that's OK. I've just spent three hours getting ready, that's all. No, you go to your precious snooker, I couldn't care less. Well, Andy never does that to Carol. They're always together. In fact I heard they're getting engaged. No-one'll want to marry you, though, you mark my words!"*

"And that Jane," you're busy telling a crowd of your mates, "has just got to be the biggest tart in the town. I mean she was all *over* Billy at the disco on Saturday, not to mention John and David and Kev . . . "

Suddenly you notice your mates' fixed expressions. Are they bored? you wonder. Why are they gazing over your shoulder? It couldn't . . . no, it wouldn't be . . . naw, Jane *couldn't* have just

appeared behind you, could she? Could she?
Yup!

WHAT YOU SHOULD SAY:
"Don't you agree, Jane? Oh, of course, you don't know Jane Jones, do you? She lives at the other side of town . . . "

WHAT YOU DO SAY: *"Oh, hello Jane! We were just talking about — er — we were . . . What? Did I call you what? No, Jane, not me, really! Why would I say anything like that about you?"*

You've been kept in *again* — if it's not detention it's hockey practice. As you're walking up the road all on your own, you hear a yell, and the sexiest beast in the school runs up and starts to chat. Unfortunately, he's just a mate, and he just happens to be going out with Battling Bertha, the baddest bitch on the block.

The two of you are wandering along having a heart to heart when — yup, you guessed it — who appears on the horizon but Bertha herself! You know it's perfectly innocent, he knows it's perfectly innocent, but how are you going to convince her?

WHAT YOU SHOULD SAY:
Nothing. Let him do the talking. He's cool enough to handle this, and besides, he's not scared of her.

WHAT YOU DO SAY: *"Hallo, Bertha. Now before you say anything, I know what you're thinking, but I can assure you it's nothing like . . . Now Bertha, Bertha, let's not be hasty . . . Bertha . . . Yeooowwch!"*

"No, this time it's for real," you're telling your mates. "I'm in love. He's beautiful! Yeah, it's Stevie. When I look into his big blue eyes I just go weak at the knees." Just at this moment, the man himself comes round the corner, in time to hear you say, "and it goes without saying he must be the best kisser in the school. And his bum! He's definitely got the best bum I've ever seen."

Wondering why your mates are having hysterics, you look over your shoulder to see Stevie grinning like a maniac. Oh the embarrassment! You'll never live this down! He's just going to think you're a lovestruck kid. He'll never look at you now. Oh woe!

WHAT YOU SHOULD SAY:
"Well, go on — aren't you going to prove it? That you're the best kisser, I mean . . . "

WHAT YOU DO SAY: *"I don't know what you're grinning at, Steven, I wasn't talking about you. No-one in their right mind could fancy you! I didn't mean you! I'm not kidding! I mean it . . . "*

back to the

FUTURE

Fashion has changed a lot over the years — some of it attractive, some not so attractive!

But even if you don't fancy wearing a complete Flapper outfit, there are lots of styles and accessories you can borrow from any past era wh will look just as good today.

THE *Twenties were the age of the movie and everyone wanted to look like a film star . . .*
The stars of the time had to wear very heavy make-up so that even movie-goers at the back of the cinema could see their expressions.

The results of this were that the Twenties flapper girl went totally overboard with cosmetics, using thick black kohl to make her eyes look rounder and bright red lipstick to paint on a 'Cupid's Bow'.

Hairstyles were the shortest they'd ever been with two very popular styles — a very short bob and the Eton crop, which was similar to our model's hair.

A flat chest was a great advantage — well endowed girls felt forced into bandaging their chests to create the ironing board front. For those whose waists were rather more than waspish, the twenties caused no problems. Sashes were tied around the hips rather than the waist — so the odd cream cake wouldn't show up.

To recreate the twenties look for parties, old satin nightdresses teamed with long beads and feathers or long tunics over longer skirts sashed at the hip should give an authentic look. Long evening gloves and beaded scarves are lucky jumble sale finds to complete the image.

26

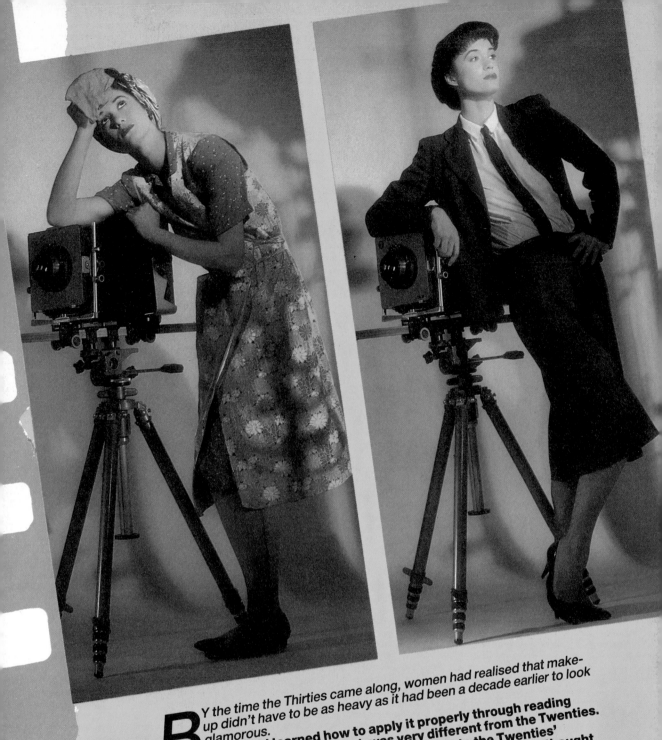

BY the time the Thirties came along, women had realised that make-up didn't have to be as heavy as it had been a decade earlier to look glamorous.

They'd learned how to apply it properly through reading women's magazines and the look was very different from the Twenties. Eyes were more subtle, and in total contrast to the Twenties' 'Cupid's Bow' — the larger your mouth, the better. If a woman thought her mouth too small she simply obliterated it with heavy 'pan-stick' make-up and 'painted' on a bigger one!

Hair styles were longer, but often rolled up or pinned into curls for a more glamorous look (or to keep it out of the way of war-effort work).

During the Thirties and Forties Britain had to face depression and war. Along with food and other necessities, clothes were rationed and people were forced to fall back on resourcefulness in order to make ends meet. Clothes were cut on narrower lines to save on material and suits became rather military looking and often rather plain. To preserve clothes, aprons and headscarves became more noticeable in factories and in the home, and precious outfits saved up for with ration coupons were saved for Saturday nights. If nylons weren't available, tea was used to stain the legs, and your best mate would have to draw a 'seam' down the back of your leg with an eye pencil — so we weren't the first generation to use leg make-up!

27

INSTEAD of film stars, rock singers were the new heroes and the Fifties was the decade of the teenager.

Make-up became stronger again with very dark painted-on eyebrows and the famous 'doe-eyed' look — where liquid eyeliner was painted on to the top lid following the line of the eyelashes and winging out at the sides. Faces were very pale and lips were bright and glossy.

Teenagers loved easy-to-care-for styles, away from the fussy look of the war years and a ponytail was probably the most popular style around.

Dancing under the mirror lights at the local dance-hall must have been an uncomfortable business when winkle pickers were the only shoes fit to be seen in. Old stone and wooden floors still bear the scars of countless stillettoes that clicked their way around the world of the Fifties. The hour-glass figure became a must, and if you didn't fit the bill, you could squeeze your way into a tight-fitting corset and stuff Kleenex down your front. Dance dresses were swirly and bright with miles of netting underskirts to make them stand out in the crowd.

Clean-cut bobby-soxers could be seen sipping Coke at the local coffee bar, where they listened to American juke-box songs and discussed the latest ski-pants and compared the length of their ponytails.

THE only natural thing about Sixties style was bare feet (ask your mum about Sandie Shaw) and long hair, but even that was heavily hairsprayed.

Sixties faces were well-covered and big expressive eyes were emphasised with half-moon eyebrows and plenty of eyeliner. What you lacked in lashes you could stick on with a bit of glue. Lips were thick and very pale, and face painting was an optional extra.

Mini-skirts, flares and floppy hats were 'groovy' and the more garish the colour, the better. Anything made of plastic was cool, and trendy girls got their mums to crochet bright tank-tops and waistcoats for them.

1. Your mother refuses to let you st
out later than 10 o'clock. But you've
been invited to a Christmas party th
won't end until midnight. How do yo
extend your deadline?
a) Get all your mates to come round a
plead for you, telling your mum that
they've all got permission.
b) Shout over your shoulder, as you'r
leaving to go to the party "Oh, by the
way, mum, expect me home at
midnight!".
c) Tell her that a fleet of taxis has bee
booked to ferry everyone home at
exactly midnight. (It hasn't, but you
know your mate's dad will give you a
d) Plead very sweetly and humbly, an
if possible, squeeze a couple of tears
out.

2. Your boyfriend has football on
Saturday mornings, but *this* Saturd
there's a day outing to London
organised by your mum's work, and
you want him to come with you, so
you won't have to tramp round the
Tower of London with all the old
couples. How do you persuade him
come?
a) Put a notice on the football
noticeboard saying that Saturday's
match is cancelled.
b) Ask him straight out to choose: you
football.
c) Give him a special present: a ticket
Arsenal's home match, that day.
d) Explain the situation to him, and be
him to make up his own mind, but telli
him you've already talked one of the
other lads into substituting for him this
week.

3. You discover, to your horror, tha
you and your mate have just bought
the same dress to wear at Saturday
disco. How do you persuade her to
trade hers in for something else?
a) Cry, while explaining that your little

32

BEASTLY!

DO you usually manage to get your own way?

Most of us do, in the long run! But the way

you do it says a lot about your hidden animal

instincts. Our quiz will bring out the beast in

you . . .

gran spent the whole of that week's pension money on the dress, and picked it out for you specially because it was the same colour as your grandad's eyes.
b) Say, "Well, I have to admit that it shows off your panty-line beautifully."
c) Argue the point until you've both reached some sort of agreement — you persuade her, quite reasonably, that she looks like a dying Christmas tree in the dress!
d) Tell her you're going to the disco in the dress. She can please herself whether she does as well.

4. Your mate who works in the record store tells you your mum's just bought you a Madonna album as a surprise pressie. Nice thought, Mum, but you'd rather have U2. How do you suggest she's made a gaffe?
a) Go on, loudly, while you're both doing the washing up, about how some grannies at your school actually like that sick Madonna rubbish, but how you told them, in no uncertain terms, that U2 is the sound of the future . . .
b) Find the album in your mum's secret hiding-place, and lean it up against the nearest radiator.
c) Don't say anything. Accept the record and swap it the next day.
d) Whisper to her, when you've made her a nice cup of tea, "D'you think you could lend me the money to buy the new U2 album? I want it more than anything in the whole world."

5. You've heard a rumour that your best mate's after your boyfriend. She's not going to have him. You put a stop to that by . . .
a) inviting her to a "fancy dress" party at your house, making sure she's the only one who thinks it's fancy dress, and suggest she wears that wonderful banana outfit she wore at last year's Town Carnival contest.

b) nuzzling up to your boyfriend's ear and whispering softly in it, "You know my mate with the bad breath and the acne? She reckons she can make you fall for her."
c) grabbing her in the playground and telling her to lay off, or else . . .
d) inviting her for coffee with the two of you, and then saying, "Right, Deirdre, I've heard you fancy Simon. Simon, what do you think of her? Do you fancy her? Or do you think it's a bit off for a best mate to go round trying to nick other people's boyfriends? Suggests she can't get one of her own, doesn't it?" etc. etc.

6. The Party of the Year's being held on Saturday by this hunk who hardly knows you exist except in school uniform so he hasn't invited you. How do you get there?
a) Gatecrash.
b) Snuggle up to his spotty friend so obviously that spotty friend invites you. You can alway leave him in the front porch once you get there.
c) Phone the hunk and ask him whether you're allowed to bring a friend to the party as well. When he asks who you are, tell him your name and say, "Don't you remember? The one you met at the disco/gym/party last week". Because he can only hear your voice and can't see you, he won't be able to remember whether he did meet you or not. Easy!
d) Ask him if you can come round to help cut the sandwiches. Then wink, ever so slowly.

Scoring

Circle the number next to your answer.
Question 1
a) 1 b) 4 c) 2 d) 3
Question 2
a) 2 b) 4 c) 3 d) 1
Question 3
a) 3 b) 2 c) 1 d) 4

Question 4
a) 1 b) 2 c) 4 d) 3
Question 5
a) 2 b) 3 c) 4 d) 1
Question 6
a) 4 b) 2 c) 1 d) 3

Analysis

Mostly 1. You're a monkey. You get out of everything with a bit of chat, and a bit more, and a bit more . . . You believe that everything can be solved by a good heart-to-heart talk, a sensible discussion or a few wise-cracks. Unfortunately, sometimes, you talk yourself into more trouble than you talk yourself out of. And you're not the most tactful person in the world!

Mostly 2. You're a snake. Quite honestly, you'll lie and cheat, tell whoppers, do the dirty, and speak with forked tongue to get your own way. Often you get away with it because you move in so silently and strike so quickly that no-one knows what's hit them until they're down. But an awful lot of people recognise a snake when they see one, and run away. And some people never recover from snake-bites, but others live to tell the tale . . .

Mostly 3. You're a pussycat. Sweet, gentle and so purringly loveable that butter wouldn't melt in your mouth. You can make yourself so adorable, and so big-eyed and lonesome, that everyone wants to take you in and cuddle you. Eventually, of course, they discover you've got very sharp claws!

Mostly 4. You're a bull. Head down, you go crashing in without a care in the world and trample on everything that gets in your way. You believe that the no-nonsense approach is the best, and charge in with the least provocation. Unfortunately you don't pick and choose where you trample, and all sorts of people can get hurt. Including you, in the end.

Dear Santa,

continued from page 21
I didn't have to turn my head to know that Somebody had just walked in. Her smile was neon-lit.

"Well, would you just believe who's here," she murmured.

"I don't need three guesses, thanks," I replied, but she wasn't listening. She kind of drifted past me like a wind through grass and made for the door.

I turned slowly. Sure enough Danny was there — relaxed and smiling as ever — but his eyes were watchful, and, just behind him, half in the shadow, stood a pretty blonde haired girl all in black.

"Hi, Becky," I heard him say as she materialised in front of him. "Sorry we're late. We got held up . . . oh, by the way,

this is Kathy. I don't think you've met."

I would have laughed at the expression on Becky's face if I hadn't been feeling so completely suicidal myself.

Sunday 21st December

Last night's disco didn't rate as the best night of my entire life but it had its moments. The worst was watching Danny dance with Kathy: they moved so beautifully it was obvious they loved dancing together and must have done it a lot. When he came over eventually and asked me to dance I felt like I had both feet embedded in concrete.

"Things don't change much round here," said Danny, holding me lightly. It was a slow, smoochy number and he was close enough for me to count the pale freckles across his nose. "You and Becky for instance. You were best friends when we were in Mrs Cooper's class."

"Were we? I suppose we must have been. It's such a long time ago."

"I remember it like it was yesterday," he smiled. "You whipping smoothly through your Gold Book Eight and me with my jaws clamped together dreading it being my turn to read. D . . . D . . . Danny, you called me."

"Did I? Did we?" I felt hot with embarrassment again. "How foul. But you don't stammer any more."

"No. Well, only now and then. When I'm dead nervous. The people who fostered me sent me to a speech therapist."

"And it worked? Well, obviously it worked." I was answering my own questions now.

"It helped. That, and being away from my old man."

I struggled to frame a polite reply. "Is your father out of prison now?" seemed less than tactful.

"How long have you been — er — fostered?" I asked. Why did I manage to make it sound like a social disease? He didn't seem to notice.

"Since I was nine. They came to the Children's Home. It's a bit like going to the R.S.P.C.A. for a puppy — and I was the little runt of the litter who took their fancy." His blue eyes glinted with mockery at my pained expression. "Don't worry. I was lucky. It's been roses all the way ever since."

"Oh, *good*," I gushed. Who *was* this brainless female wittering on like a lady Conservative candidate? I put it down to lightheadedness brought on by my recent brush with death. Either that or Danny Kelly's mouth being close enough to kiss. Whatever it was I'd made the biggest mess ever of our first proper conversation.

The music stopped and we stood for a second looking at each other and I had this wild hope. He'll say, "Can I see you tomorrow?" or, "Don't worry about Kathy. She's just an old friend."

He didn't say anything like that at all. He put his hand out and touched the silver chain round my neck. "You still wear it then," was all he said. Next minute he'd disappeared and I was standing like a lost umbrella waiting to be found.

It rained all day today.

I think I'm starting a cold.

Tuesday 23rd December

Waved to Danny this morning from my bedroom window. He waved back. Thought about that odd remark of his about my silver chain . . .

Suddenly it all came back to me and I sat down with a thud on my bed. How could I have forgotten it? We were all lined up in the Hall, Junior One in the front row and Mr Sanders towering over us like a great black crow . . .

"Someone has stolen Suzanne Davidson's silver chain. I will find the culprit if it's the last thing I do!" he snarled. "In fact, I have a very good idea who that culprit is."

Silence. We stood like statues as his eyes searched up and down the rows of children like laser beams, finally fixing, inevitably, on Danny Kelly.

"I have *proof*," lowering his voice to a Vincent Price hiss, "and I will not hesitate to hand that proof to the Proper Authorities . . ." All eyes turned to Danny. His face was white as paper and there was a thin film of sweat dampening his forehead under his dusty hair . . . "the Police and, of course, the culprit's father."

Danny wet his lips. Did Mr Sanders *know* about the belts Danny got from his dad? We'd seen the bruises in P.E. Surely he wouldn't' . . . I put my hand up.

"Yes, Suzanne?"

"Please, sir, about my silver chain. My mum found it this morning, sir, in a drawer. She said to tell you."

I don't remember if he really believed me. I only remember the lie and the look

of relief on Danny Kelly's face. It must have been soon after that the Kellys left because that same night there was an envelope pushed under our door with my chain inside it and then I forgot all about it. Until now.

I phoned Becky to see if she remembered the drama.

"Vaguely," she said. "They were all tea-leaves, the Kellys. The eldest nicked the wheels off Mr Sanders car once. Don't you remember . . ."

She went rabbitting on but I wasn't listening. I don't care what anybody says, I still reckon Danny never stole my chain in the first place.

Wednesday 24th December

I met him in town. Outside MacDonalds.

"Suzi!" he said. "The very girl."

I poised myself expectantly. For what was I the very girl?

"Have you half an hour to spare?"

I had the rest of my life if he cared to make use of it. I consulted my Swatch. "I think so. I just have a bit of Christmas shopping to do." Dad had passed me a couple of crisp blue notes that morning which were about to make all the difference to my seasonal offerings.

"A coffee first." He pushed me into the cafe and ordered two coffees in nothing flat. I was still unwinding my scarf when he leaned towards me.

"It's Kathy," he said. My warm bubble of happiness burst immediately. "I can't think what to buy her for Christmas and I'm sure you'll be able to help."

"What makes you so sure? I hardly know her," I protested weakly.

"You'll think of something." He fixed me with that devastating blue gaze. "Kathy's . . . well, she's sort of special. You understand."

"Oh, yes," I nodded, fighting down the great big lump of disappointment that threatened to choke me. Damn Kathy. May she wake up on Christmas Day with a big red spot on the end of her perfect nose!

He leaned back smiling his gentle, charming smile. So cool, so smooth. It was incredible how much he'd changed from that terrified little boy . . .

"I'd forgotten that business about my silver chain," I said, suddenly, before I could stop myself.

"Had you? I hadn't." He didn't appear at all bothered, thank goodness.

"I didn't steal it, you know. Oh, I had it alright but I actually found it in the playground. I knew it was yours." He paused, a far-away look coming over his face. "I remember thinking, 'I'll tell Suzi I've found her chain and she'll be dead grateful.' I don't know why it was so important to me that you'd be grateful but it was. Perhaps because you were so posh . . ." He paused teasingly . . . "or so pretty."

"You must have had it quite a while," I persisted, pretending to ignore the fact that I was having a major coronary because he'd said I was pretty.

"I think I did. I hid it. I was fascinated by the shininess and the feel of it. But I didn't intend keeping it, honestly."

"I believe you." I did too. I could just imagine him gazing at the chain the way he gazed at my apple and my reading book and everything else he didn't think he'd ever have.

"You got me out of big trouble," he grinned.

"Which reminds me, you're helping me choose a present. Come on."

We wandered around for a little while looking at this and that and niffing the free perfume samples and ended up, eventually, outside a big jewellers where I knew they sold really pretty bracelets and rings.

"Don't let him want to get her a ring," I prayed, pressing my nose to the glass window. He settled for a bracelet — slim and very delicate, like Kathy herself.

"Thanks, Suzi," he said when we came out. "I'm sure she'll love it."

"Oh, my pleasure," I lied. "There's nothing like a surprise on Christmas morning," I added, hoping that Kathy's surprise would be to wake up and find that the Christmas tree had fallen on her head.

"What are you hoping for then?"

"Me?" I could hardly tell him my hopes had just flown out the window. "I don't know. Maybe I'll get a surprise too."

Or maybe I won't.

Thursday 25th December

Well, S. Claus did his best. Or rather Mum and Dad did. I was fairly knocked out by all the goodies they heaped on me — including a brand new camera which I'd been dying for. Becky phoned.

"Where *were* you last night? You were supposed to come to Dave's party."

"I know, I know," I sighed. "I couldn't face it. Why? Did I miss something interesting?"

"You bet you did. Danny turned up again and he had that girl with him."

"Suzi, she *is* his sister! I was right," squeaked Becky triumphantly. When was she right? She never said he'd got a sister.

"He hasn't got a sister. Brothers, yes," I replied wearily.

"I know that." She knows everything. "I'm telling you that girl Kathy is his sister — his foster sister. He lives with her

family. She told me so. She's not his girlfriend at all."

"She's still not his sister either," I said flatly. "I can't see what difference it makes."

"But . . ."

"Becky, I have to go," I interrupted. "Mum needs me to help her stuff the turkey." I put the phone down. Not his girlfriend? Huh! Becky could jump to a conclusion faster than a frog could spit.

"Suzanne," called Mum. "There's someone at the door for you." The someone stepped in. "Happy Christmas, Mrs Davidson," he murmured, politely.

She hadn't a clue. "It's Danny, Mum."

"Oh. Happy Christmas, Danny." From the look on her face I could tell she thought the change was for the better but she was still a long way from approving of anyone called Kelly.

I grabbed his arm. "Come and look at our tree. It's really great," I said, propelling him swiftly into the living room.

"Magic," he said as I scrabbled about under the needle-sharp branches finding the plug for the fairy lights.

"There," I breathed, jumping up and standing back to admire the effect, because I'm crazy about Christmas trees all lit up. Only I trod on Danny's foot and we both collapsed onto the sofa in a fairly untidy heap.

"Magic," repeated Danny, not looking at the tree at all.

"Did Kathy like her bracelet?" I asked, untangling myself from his sweater.

"Oh, yes. She liked it a lot. She said to tell you thanks for helping choose it. She knows I'm useless at making my mind up. Which reminds me . . ." He held out a small, shiny gold parcel.

"Oh." I was pretty dumbstruck but I managed to claw my way through the paper and ribbon to a beautiful pair of silver earrings . . . "Oh, Danny."

"Kathy helped me choose them," he confessed, "but I said I wanted something to go with your chain."

"Oh, Danny." I couldn't think of anything else to say. He was looking at me with that longing expression in his eyes, the one he reserved for things he thought he'd never get, and I knew for certain that he never looked that way at Kathy. "But I haven't got any present for you. That's awful."

He put his arms round me. "Remember that day you came in the shop to buy Christmas cards?"

I nodded. I could see a tiny image of myself in the blue depths of his eyes.

"Well, I looked at you and I thought — Danny, you've been a good lad all year. S . . . Santa should put s . . . something special in your sock this Christmas. Like Suzi Davidson. She'd be the b . . . best present in the world."

I almost giggled. I mean, great minds think alike and all that, and I was so happy I could have floated round the room like a party balloon.

"Give me a clue then," he said, pulling me closer. "S . . . say something."

"Merry Christmas, Danny," I whispered, in between kissing the mouth I'd been longing to kiss for days and days, "and a very happy New Year."

SWEET I

Just because I dress a little differently didn't mean my mum should pick on me all the time. She was ruining my confidence — and I needed all the confidence I could find if I was to make an impression on Dave . . .

M UM'S angry voice made me freeze in the doorway. "Have you any idea at all what you look like?"

I didn't turn round. I knew she'd be glaring, and the voice was enough without having to meet her furious eyes.

"A bundle of rags, that's what you look like! A dirty bundle, at that."

"They're perfectly clean!" I was stung into replying. "I washed everything myself — except the boots, of course." I glanced down at the tiny Edwardian-style boots with their shiny buttons; fifty pence they'd cost me. An absolute gift. Of course most people's feet were far too huge to fit them . . .

"But *why*? For heaven's sake, Anne, why do you have to keep buying those dreadful clothes from flea markets when I'm perfectly willing to buy you proper, modern clothes? Pretty, modern clothes.

"Why can't you be like your friends? I saw Lorna yesterday in the loveliest pink leggings and brightly coloured shirt. She looked super."

Of course she did, I thought. She's tall and attractive — like you are. I'm four foot eleven in my socks, and if I wore Lorna's clothes I'd look like a mobile mushroom. I chewed my lip and gazed over her shoulder. She'd stop in a while . . .

"And Louise too. Even though she isn't pretty she looks bright and interesting. A bit way out, perhaps, but at least she's not wandering about in somebody else's cast-offs."

Louise is going to be a designer when she leaves school. She makes herself the most amazing things, really unusual, and she couldn't care less about other people's opinions. Louise has bags of confidence.

So has my mother.

I sighed. "Can I go now?"

"I don't know why I waste my breath," she muttered, letting go of my arm and looking round for her bag. "Yes, of course you can go. And don't forget your key. I'm taking Stevie to the dentist and we may be late back." She patted my hand and I remembered thinking what a fantastic shade of nail varnish she was wearing. It matched her skirt. She was always colour-matched, my mum, like somebody out of a magazine.

"I'll get tea ready," I said, anxious as usual not to part on bad terms. I didn't want to upset her that much anyway. It wasn't her fault she couldn't understand . . .

"Thanks. It's only salad. If you just set the table and . . ." Her voice trailed away and she looked at me sadly. "I'm sorry, Annie. I shouldn't be so critical, I suppose. I don't mean to be nasty but . . ."

"It's OK, Mum," I said quickly. I didn't want her to start rabbiting on about what good friends we used to be and how she knew it was difficult in your teens and all that rubbish. We'd done that scene about a million times. "I really do have to go. Louise is meeting me on the two o'clock bus. 'Bye!"

I nearly fell on my face trying to make the bus-stop because my lace petticoat insisted on winding itself round my knees so I was lucky to leap on board at the last minute.

"You looked like Eliza Doolittle doing the four-minute mile," giggled Lou as I sank breathlessly into the seat next to her.

"Don't you start," I gasped. "I've had enough earache for one day."

"Your mum again?" Louise was immediately sympathetic.

"Who else? She wants to know why I don't look bright and interesting like you do."

"Bright!" Louise spluttered. "Interesting! I sound like Postman Pat."

"It was supposed to be a compliment." I glanced at Louise's buttercup yellow hair and eyes painted like giant moths. "Anything's better than a daughter who looks like she's fallen off a stall at a jumble sale."

"How mean. You don't look like that at all," said Louise, loyally. "Why can't your mum see that people have to develop their own personalities? She might look great in her way, but it's not *yours*. Your ideas are original. Different. She'd have us all going around like sheep."

REEDOM

"David Chester," I said. I could feel my face reddening. "He's that boy who started last term. Right at the end. Don't you remember him barging into our English class by mistake?"

"I remember. I thought he seemed familiar." She twisted her neck to gaze at him as the bus lurched forward. "I wonder if he ever found Room Eight?"

"Come on. It's our stop."

We clattered downstairs and jumped on to the pavement. Louise turned immediately in the direction of the record shop.

"I thought we were going for shoes for you?" I reminded her.

"We are. But first I need to get that Frankie album for your birthday," she grinned. "They may be sold out by next Tuesday."

"Some birthday surprise I'm going to get," I muttered, trudging after her through the crowd.

"Stop moaning and come on."

He was standing by the counter rifling through some singles as we went in and he might not have noticed us if Louise hadn't managed to trip over his feet.

"I'm sorry," he said (though it wasn't his fault). "Are you OK?"

"Yes, fine. Really," she breathed, widening the moth-eyes and smiling.

"It's David, isn't it?"

"Yes." He looked at both of us uncertainly. "Haven't I seen you in school? I've met so many people lately I'm afraid I still get half their names mixed up . . ."

"We haven't actually met," Louise said, "but we've seen you around. I'm Louise and this is Anne."

"Hi," he smiled. He had a lovely smile. "Well, er, how about coming for a coffee now we've been introduced and all that? If you've finished in here, that is."

"That would be great, wouldn't it, Annie? We didn't come in for anything special, did we?"

"Nothing that won't be sold out by next Tuesday," I muttered. She wasn't listening. She was too busy fascinating David to hear me and I was, suddenly, too depressed to care. I trailed after them to a café and sat there feeling like a gooseberry, all small and sour, and I knew I was being silly really. Nobody had stitched my mouth up or told me not to

compete with Louise for David's attention. I just didn't. I drank my coffee and picked at the yellow silk of my shawl and wished I were dead.

"He's going to the disco on Saturday," announced Lou on the way home. She looked like she'd swallowed a plate of strawberries. "I'm going to make something really stunning to wear. What about you?"

"What about me?"

"Oh, come on, Annie. You're coming, aren't you? David did ask you if you were, you know, but you didn't say anything. I mean at this stage there's no knowing who he fancies. Say you'll come."

I said I'd think about it. I knew she meant what she said. Louise wasn't the type who'd deliberately try and cut you out with a boy because it was all a big laugh with her; she just liked to flirt and have fun, and she'd no idea how I felt about him. She didn't know that just to look at him made my insides turn to jelly. All that week I kept imagining how fantastic it would be if I went and he danced with me . . .

"I'm going to Auntie Gwen's on Saturday night," said Mum over breakfast on Friday, "but your dad's staying in so he'll see to Stevie if you want to go out."

"Right," I said. I wasn't very interested.

"This disco that Louise keeps phoning about . . ." She paused. "Will you be going?"

"Why?" I said, focusing slowly.

"Oh, nothing. I just wondered. Only it's your birthday on Tuesday and I thought you might like a new . . ."

"No thanks," I said quickly. "I doubt I'll go anyway so don't be worrying that I'll look like Cinderella at the ball and let you down."

She went a bit pink. Dad said quietly, "There's no need to snap, Anne. Your mother only wants you to look nice."

I got up. "I *do* look nice! Look at me!" My voice was rising hysterically. "Don't I look nice?" I twirled round and round in my grey school skirt and white blouse. "Don't I look neat and sweet and clean?"

"Don't be silly, Anne," he frowned. "Sit down and eat your breakfast."

"Why? If I eat all my toast will it make me a big girl? Will I ever

"Some sheep look pretty good though, don't they?" I sighed. "Lorna, for instance."

"Lorna would look good in prison underwear with a bucket on her head!" Louise snapped. "You should stop comparing yourself all the time. You're always putting yourself down."

"I'm not!" I protested. "It's not easy trying to do your own thing when you're lumbered with a mother who looks like she's walked off the set of 'Dallas'."

"And keeps trying to cast you as the Poison Dwarf," giggled Louise. "Right."

We both stared glumly ahead for a while. I'd just thought of something else I wanted to tell her when she dug me sharply in the ribs and pointed out of the window.

"See that boy over there? The dark-haired one outside the record shop. Isn't he called David something or other?"

grow? Or will I always look twelve years old? Even out of uniform I do. And when I wear the clothes I like, *she* says I look like a tramp as well!"

I ran out of the room, tears streaming down my face. Up in the bathroom I could hear their voices rising and falling, concerned. I splashed some cold water on my face and peered at myself in the mirror. "It's not fair. Why should I be the one left behind? If I couldn't get to be tall at least I could have some *shape*!" I tucked my blouse savagely inside my skirt and dragged my belt tight. I still had hips like a boy. No wonder all the boys in my year treated me like a pal — they probably hadn't noticed the difference. As for pulling David . . . there was no chance . . .

I saw him in the corridor that morning. I was just asking one of the second year kids if Mr Benson had sorted out the swimming teams for the gala when David came out of Room Eight.

"Hi, Anne." He stopped and smiled at me. My mouth went quite dry. "Oh, hi, David. Are you still going tomorrow? Louise says they've booked a good band."

He nodded. "And you? You're coming, aren't you?"

"I — er, I don't know. Maybe."

He frowned and seemed about to say more but the kid butted in with some lists she'd fished out of her grotty bag and the bell went. He wandered off but he looked over his shoulder a couple of times. I nearly melted into the ground.

"It's what to wear if I do go," I sighed.

"What about that lace camisole top you found at your grans'?" said Lorna, flapping her nails. "You could gel your hair too. It would make you look older."

"An elderly thirteen, you mean?" I sniffed. We were supposed to be revising French in the library. Louise looked up from the sketch of some shorts she was designing on the back of her Rough book.

"For goodness sake snap out of it, Annie. You're acting like wet fog. It's not Lorna's fault she's been taken for Kate Bush since she was nine so stop scowling at her."

"Sorry. I can't help wondering what it must be like to be glamorous, that's all."

"I'll make you glamorous if you're that keen. I'll come round tomorrow, before the disco, and do your eye make-up. You'll look fantastic."

"I'll look like a very tired panda if you do it like you did the last time . . ."

Then I ducked to avoid one

French dictionary and a bottle of nail varnish being hurled at my head.

Lorna and Louise weren't the only people determined to help. When I went up to my room on Saturday there was a dress hanging outside the wardrobe and a note from Mum. Typical, I thought. She just can't stop poking her nose in; trying to make me into somebody I'm not . . . as if I'd wear her taste in dresses. I picked up the note reluctantly and frowned over it.

"Dear Anne, Please give the dress a chance. Try it on. It's an un-birthday present in case you decide to go to the disco. Don't be cross. With love from your interfering Mum."

Oh, Mum! I thought, feeling guilty. I took the dress from the hanger; it was dark and silky and straight. Different. I hesitated. Perhaps, for once, Mum had thought about what might suit *me* instead of what looked good on my friends or what she liked herself.

SWEET FREEDOM

I tried it. The effect was quite startling. It didn't exactly give me curves but it certainly clung to what shape there was.

Louise thought so too when she arrived. She couldn't wait to start doing my make-up but I made her do it like I wanted it, not vivid but kind of smudgy and subtle. When she finished and slicked my hair I reckoned that, with the dress and fairly high heels I could have passed for seventeen easily. Well, in a bad light. I picked up my yellow shawl and looked at Louise hesitantly. "What d'you think?"

"Oh, yes. It's just what that dress needs," she said. "It sets it off. Besides, it's great to mix up old and new things."

I felt OK, then. Wearing Mum's choice of dress and using Lou's help was fine as long as I could add a bit of me.

What would David think, though? I was so nervous I could hardly speak. Suppose he didn't notice me? Suppose he

preferred Louise in her emerald green shorts and backless (and almost frontless) T-shirt?

"Every girl for herself," giggled Lou as we pushed our way through the crowd. The music was pounding out and I could see Lorna dancing with three boys under a flickering spotlight, but I couldn't see David.

"Hi, Louise. Have you seen Anne? I've been looking all over but — hey, it's you!"

"Of course it's me." I pretended to be indignant. "Anybody would think I had two heads or something."

He smiled delightedly. "Oh no — not *two* heads."

There was a small silence.

"Well, you thrashed that one out between you," remarked Louise, looking from David to me and back again. "Now what?"

"Now we dance," said David firmly and took my hand.

"All of us?" said Louise hopefully.

"Sorry, Louise."

She grinned cheerfully. "You realise this could ruin my confidence; I'll probably end up with an inferiority complex and it will be all your fault . . ."

"She'll end up with Gareth Scott more likely," said David, pulling me close to him. "He's been waiting to get his chance with her for ages they tell me."

I came out from my dreamy trance long enough to be glad that Louise wasn't really upset and wouldn't be on her own for long, then I simply drifted back. We moved slowly to the beat of the music and my head rested comfortably on his shoulder so he wasn't that much taller than me . . .

"I've been a bit of a wally," he said, after a long time. "I've been thinking about you non-stop since last Saturday. I was hoping you'd come tonight but you didn't seem too keen and then . . ."

"Go on, admit it — you thought I was a Second Year, didn't you?"

"No! At least, not for long. I asked around, didn't I? I mean I was fairly depressed thinking I'd have to hang about waiting till you got a bit older . . ."

I couldn't tell if he was teasing me or not. "Don't tell me you were prepared to wait," I mocked, "because I don't believe it."

"Don't. But it's true." He pulled me closer. "Anyway it doesn't matter — not if we both feel the same way . . .?"

I leaned back and looked into his eyes. They were hazel flecked with greenish-gold. He had freckles on his nose. I wanted to tell him but there was this stupid lump in my throat so I did the only thing left to do and kissed him.

LOVE CAN'T TURN AROUND

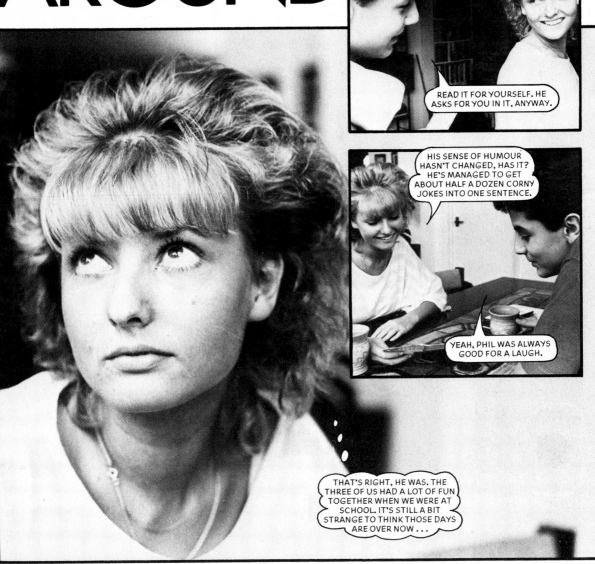

John, Maggie and Phil had been the best of pals all through their schooldays . . .

I MIGHT'VE KNOWN YOU THREE WOULD BE TOGETHER, AS USUAL. DIDN'T YOU HEAR THE BELL FOR THE AFTERNOON CLASS?

SORRY, SIR. WE WERE SO BUSY TALKING, WE FORGOT ABOUT THE TIME . . .

It was a friendship that nothing and no one could spoil . . .

I WISH I'D TWO BLOKES HANGING ROUND ME ALL THE TIME, LIKE YOU HAVE. THEY'RE BOTH NICE, TOO. I'M NOT SURPRISED YOU CAN'T DECIDE WHICH ONE YOU LIKE BEST!

IT ISN'T LIKE THAT, ALICE. THE THREE OF US ARE MATES, THAT'S ALL. THERE'S NO ROMANCE IN IT.

GO ON — YOU'RE NOT GOING TO TELL ME YOU DON'T SECRETLY FANCY ONE OF THEM!

WELL, IT'S TRUE. THE THREE OF US GET ON GREAT TOGETHER. BUT THAT'S THE WHOLE POINT — WE'RE A THREESOME, NOT A TWOSOME . . .

Then, just before they left school, Phil's family decided to emigrate to Australia . . .

DON'T WORRY, YOU TWO HAVEN'T HEARD THE LAST OF ME. I'LL BE WRITING NEARLY EVERY WEEK TO GIVE YOU ALL THE NEWS.

YOU'D BETTER SEND THE LETTERS TO ME, THEN, IF YOU WANT A REPLY YOU CAN READ. NEITHER OF US HAS EVER BEEN ABLE TO MAKE ANY SENSE OUT OF MAGGIE'S SCRAWL!

CHEEK. MY WRITING ISN'T THAT BAD!

That had been nearly two months ago — and now . . .

PHIL CERTAINLY SEEMS TO BE ENJOYING HIMSELF, DOESN'T HE? I'M GLAD HE KEPT HIS PROMISE TO WRITE AND LET US KNOW WHAT WAS HAPPENING.

YEAH, I'D HAVE HATED US TO LOSE TOUCH WITH EACH OTHER.

I'LL WRITE BACK TO PHIL THIS AFTERNOON. YOU CAN READ IT BEFORE I POST IT, IN CASE YOU WANT TO ADD A P.S OR ANYTHING. SEE YOU IN THE CAFE TONIGHT?

OK. ABOUT EIGHT O'CLOCK?

And, that night . . .

REMEMBER HOW THE THREE OF US ALWAYS USED TO COME HERE AFTER SCHOOL?

YEAH. IT'S FUNNY TO THINK THAT'S ALL FINISHED NOW, ISN'T IT? PHIL'S IN AUSTRALIA, AND THE TWO OF US HAVE LEFT SCHOOL . . .

It's funny, too, how things sometimes turn out . . .

It wasn't long before Maggie and John were going steady . . .

I USED TO TELL EVERYBODY I DIDN'T HAVE ANY ROMANTIC IDEAS ABOUT YOU, OR PHIL EITHER. I WAS WRONG, WASN'T I? I MUST HAVE SECRETLY FANCIED YOU ALL THE TIME!

MAYBE NOT. SOMETIMES FEELINGS JUST GROW, WITHOUT PEOPLE REALLY NOTICING IT.

I DON'T MIND HOW YOU FELT ABOUT ME BEFORE. AS LONG AS YOU FANCY ME NOW, THAT'S ALL THAT MATTERS.

YOU KNOW I DO, YOU IDIOT . . .

Maggie was happy, except for one thing . . .

IT SEEMS LIKE WEEKS SINCE WE HEARD FROM PHIL. DIDN'T HE REPLY TO YOUR LAST LETTER?

NO . . . NO, I HAVEN'T HEARD ANYTHING FROM HIM . . .

I SUPPOSE PHIL'S BEEN TOO BUSY TO WRITE. HE'S PROBABLY FOUND HIMSELF A GIRLFRIEND OUT THERE IN AUSTRALIA AND SHE'LL BE TAKING UP ALL HIS TIME . . .

Then one day in town . . .

HELLO, MAGGIE. I HAVEN'T SEEN YOU FOR A WHILE.

OH, IT'S PHIL'S AUNT. I WONDER IF SHE'S HEARD ANYTHING FROM HIM RECENTLY . . .?

I EXPECT YOU'LL BE LOOKING FORWARD TO SEEING PHIL WHEN HE GETS HOME. IT'S NEXT WEEK THEY'RE DUE BACK, ISN'T IT?

PHIL'S COMING HOME? FOR A HOLIDAY, YOU MEAN?

NO, FOR GOOD. THINGS DIDN'T WORK OUT AS WELL IN AUSTRALIA AS HIS FATHER HAD HOPED, SO THEY'RE COMING BACK TO BRITAIN. I THOUGHT HE'D HAVE LET YOU KNOW.

Maggie asked John about it later . . .

YEAH . . . NOW THAT YOU MENTION IT, I DID GET A LETTER FROM PHIL THE OTHER WEEK. I THINK HE DID SAY SOMETHING ABOUT COMING BACK HOME . . .

BUT WHY DIDN'T YOU TELL ME?

I MEANT TO, BUT IT MUST'VE SLIPPED MY MIND. I CAN'T REMEMBER EVERYTHING, CAN I?

She couldn't stop herself thinking about it . . .

IT DOESN'T MAKE SENSE FOR JOHN TO HAVE FORGOTTEN SOMETHING LIKE THAT. AND HE ALWAYS USED TO LET ME READ PHIL'S LETTERS. IF HE DIDN'T LET ME SEE THE LAST ONE, IT CAN ONLY BE BECAUSE HE DIDN'T WANT ME TO KNOW PHIL WAS COMING HOME. BUT WHY . . .?

JOHN'S BEEN ACTING A BIT FUNNY EVER SINCE HE TOLD ME ABOUT THAT LETTER. I JUST DON'T KNOW WHAT'S WRONG WITH HIM . . .

And, on the day Phil was due home . . .

JOHN ISN'T EVEN COMING TO THE AIRPORT WITH ME, TO MEET PHIL. HE SAID HE'S GOT TO WORK TODAY — BUT I'VE NEVER KNOWN HIM TO GO INTO THE OFFICE ON A SATURDAY BEFORE . . .

At the airport . . .

IT'S GREAT TO SEE YOU AGAIN, MAGGIE. ISN'T JOHN WITH YOU?

NO, HE COULDN'T MAKE IT, PHIL. BUT I'M DYING TO HEAR ALL YOUR NEWS . . .

DO YOU STILL GO TO THE YOUTH CLUB ON SATURDAY NIGHTS? MAYBE I'LL SEE JOHN THERE . . .

THAT'S A GOOD IDEA. IT'LL BE JUST LIKE OLD TIMES, WITH THE THREE OF US TOGETHER AGAIN.

I'LL GO AND SEE JOHN WHEN HE GETS HOME FROM WORK, AND LET HIM KNOW THE PLANS.

Maggie left Phil to go home with his parents — but, when she saw John later . . .

SORRY, MAGGIE, I DON'T FANCY THE YOUTH CLUB TONIGHT. YOU GO WITHOUT ME.

WHAT'RE YOU TALKING ABOUT? PHIL'S GOING TO BE THERE. DON'T YOU EVEN WANT TO SEE HIM, AFTER ALL THIS TIME?

I JUST DON'T WANT TO GO, OK? DON'T MAKE SUCH A BIG FUSS ABOUT IT!

WHAT'S GOT INTO HIM? HE'S NEVER ACTED LIKE THIS BEFORE . . .

Maggie went to the youth club on her own . . .

HI, MAGGIE. WHERE'S JOHN?

HE ISN'T COMING. I TRIED TO PERSUADE HIM, BUT HE JUST KEPT SAYING NO . . .

And . . .

They'd spoken to each other the day before Phil left . . .

KEEP AN EYE ON MAGGIE FOR ME, WILL YOU, MATE? DON'T LET HER GET TOO SERIOUS ABOUT ANYONE ELSE WHILE I'M GONE. I MIGHT BE COMING BACK SOON, AND I'M HOPING THAT BY THEN SHE'LL HAVE REALISED SHE LOVES ME . . .

DON'T WORRY, PHIL, YOU CAN COUNT ON ME. I WON'T LET ANY OTHER GUY GET NEAR HER!

I DIDN'T MEAN TO STEAL MAGGIE FROM YOU, PHIL. WE WERE JUST FRIENDS, LIKE WE'D ALWAYS BEEN . . . AND THEN IT JUST SEEMED TO GROW INTO SOMETHING MORE . . .

THAT'S WHY YOU'VE BEEN TRYING TO AVOID ME SINCE I GOT BACK, ISN'T IT? YOU'VE BEEN FEELING GUILTY . . . BUT YOU DON'T HAVE TO . . .

YOU MEAN YOU DON'T MIND ABOUT MAGGIE AND ME?

WELL . . . I WON'T SAY I DON'T FEEL A LITTLE JEALOUS. I SUPPOSE I DID STILL HOPE MAGGIE AND ME MIGHT GET TOGETHER WHEN I CAME HOME . . . BUT I'M NOT BREAKING MY HEART ABOUT IT.

I WAS OUT WITH OTHER GIRLS WHILE I WAS IN AUSTRALIA. I'VE GROWN UP A BIT, I SUPPOSE . . . AND EVEN I CAN SEE THAT YOU'VE MORE IN COMMON WITH MAGGIE THAN I EVER DID . . .

NOW, I RECKON IT'S TIME WE WERE MEETING HER AT THE YOUTH CLUB. THE THREE OF US HAVE GOT A LOT TO CATCH UP ON.

YOU'RE RIGHT. LET'S GO, MATE!

And . . .

SO YOU'RE NOT GOING TO TELL ME WHY YOU'VE BEEN ACTING SO MYSTERIOUS THESE LAST FEW DAYS?

NO, MAGGIE. IT'S A LITTLE SECRET BETWEEN PHIL AND ME . . . AND IT'S BETTER IF IT STAYS THAT WAY . . .

I DON'T REALLY UNDERSTAND WHAT'S BEEN GOING ON. I'M JUST HAPPY THAT THE THREE OF US ARE ALL FRIENDS AGAIN . . .

. . . AND THAT TWO OF US ARE MORE THAN JUST FRIENDS!

THE END

CHOICES

"Shall I wear my pink top even though it's unbelievably boring or will I put on the black slinky one that nearly got me arrested last time I wore it?" "Should I do that essay on The Migrating Habits of The Fruit Fly or go to the disco and pretend a burglar stole my homework?" "Should I go out with Mad Mike the Biker or his mate whom I don't fancy half so much but at least he won't give Mum and Dad a heart attack?"

Life is full of choices — some trivial, some a lot more serious. But the one thing they all have in common is that you, and you alone, must make them — and take the responsibility for your own decisions . . .

Most people make decisions quickly and maybe impulsively. And most of us, naturally enough, tend to take the easiest way out. But that might not always be the best way in the long term . . .

Take Naomi, for instance. Her dad was offered the choice of redundancy or moving to another branch of his firm, over a hundred miles away. For him, the choice was long-term security, and he decided that the family would move. He knew his decision wouldn't go down too well with Naomi, or her kid brother, Steve.

She rebelled immediately. "I told him I wasn't leaving my mates, my school, and my boyfriend, Chris. We had this big screaming row, and I told him, in no uncertain terms, that the only way he was going to get me to move was if he tied me up and dragged me."

That's understandable. Naomi didn't want to mess up her life, the one she'd become used to. She wanted to stay put. She wouldn't even listen to her dad's arguments about fresh starts and hope for the future. But, luckily for her, her dad was willing to listen to her point of view, and found a solution.

"He was brilliant!" Naomi said. "He arranged for me to stay in my home town, with my gran and grandad, whilst the rest of the family moved on. I could go to our new house at weekends, if I wanted to. He left it completely up to me."

So, her dad let Naomi make her own decision, to stay where she felt happiest. He knew that happiness is what you're looking for, when you make a choice.

*   *   *   *

But what happens when both the choices in front of you offer only misery?

Last summer, Jo was one of the lucky ones to find a job for after she left school. All she had to do was to pass 'O' level or CSE Grade One in four subjects, including English and Maths.

It looked easy for Jo, who was taking seven 'O' levels and two CSEs. Too easy.

Life is full of choices — and when you're faced with having to make a decision, especially one that's going to affect your whole life, taking the easy way out may not be the best thing to do . . .

Thinking she was safe, she eased up on school work, and when her results came through, she'd got only one pass, in 'O' level Biology.

"I had two choices: try to look for another job with the 'O' level I'd got, or go back to school feeling a failure. I really couldn't stand the embarrassment of going back when I'd been so smug about having a job, but I couldn't face the prospect of a job search either."

Either/or isn't too good when you can't bear doing either of the choices. But, when you land in that situation, you have got a way out. You can start looking for alternatives.

Jo, in despair, went to see the Careers Officer. And, surprisingly, she found there *was* another solution to her problem.

"She suggested that I enrolled at the local FE college, to take my 'O' levels again, and immediately I knew that was the answer. I wouldn't have to face school routines again, but I could re-take my exams.

"And there'd be new friends to make, and a new approach to 'O' level courses. I'd feel like a student, instead of a failure!

"The FE college is fantastic. I can honestly say that it's the best decision someone ever helped me to make," she said.

For Jo, and for Naomi, a solution to their problems came from someone trying to help. Asking for help, as Jo did, often sets you on the right road.

*   *   *   *

But Fiona found herself in a completely different situation when she had a decision to make. Far from helping, the adults involved just complicated the issue.

Her mum and dad were divorcing, and left it to her to decide which one she wanted to live with. They were both

staying in the same city, the family house was to be sold and each parent was going to find a new home, so Fiona couldn't even decide that she'd stay with which ever parent kept the house.

"It was an impossible decision," she says. "I was completely alone. I knew I couldn't consult either of them — for obvious reasons! — and there was no-one else who could help me make up my mind. I got on best with Dad, and Mum was really depressed and miserable, so the obvious choice was Dad.

"But he had work, and his mates, and, according to Mum, a new girlfriend. Mum was on her own.

"In the end, I went with Mum. I thought she needed me most, and I can tell you, I wasn't too pleased about feeling so responsible, and not really being able to put myself first. But there you go.

"Mum did need me, and she was so pleased that I'd decided to stay with her that she pulled herself together. She took me round flat-hunting with her, and we found this place, and decorated it ourselves. That was chaotic.

"Mum has changed completely. She's like a real mate, now, and I can talk to her for the first time in my life. That's the first big decision I ever made, and I thought I'd made the wrong one.

"But I hadn't, had I? It's turned out fantastic. I see Dad at the weekends. He's remarrying soon. I might even try matchmaking for my mum, given half a chance!"

So, Fiona ended up happy with a decision she'd made on her own, and to please someone else instead of herself. She made it because she saw that some decisions, eventually, have to be made 'for the best'. And that doesn't mean always putting yourself first, but sizing up the problem, and doing what's necessary.

In a way, that's what Naomi's dad did when he gave Naomi the option of staying with her gran. He tried to do what was best for her, hoping that it would turn out best for everyone in the long run.

"He's a clever bloke, my dad," Naomi told us. And she went on to finish her story, "He gave me time. That's really what I needed. Chris and I finished about two months after my parents moved away.

"All my mates were going steady, so I didn't see much of them once the school holidays started. And then, down in Bletchley where my family was living, I met Rick. He introduced me to all his mates, and I just didn't want to go back to Gran's.

"I'd missed Mum and Dad, even Steve, who's a pain most of the time. I wanted to be with them all again. So I moved back with my family, and I haven't regretted it for one minute!"

A The name of a well-known No 1 pop hit from a couple of years back . . .

1) This was the first No. 1 hit for EastEnders' Wicksy . . .

2) Nutty boys from London's Camden Town who all showed signs of complete and utter . . .

3) 'Lean On Me' and 'For America' were two hits for this bobby duo . . .

4) The biggest hit from The Human League's 'Dare' . . .

5) A dancefloor classic from The Gap Band that always has everyone upside and sitting down . . .

6) The singing debut of the guy from the Levi's ad . . .

7) Messrs. Johnson, Rutherford, O'Toole, Nash and Gill . . .

FEEDBACK SPECIAL

Yow, it's Feedback time again. But, of course, because this is an annual, there's no money up for grabs this time — just lots of opportunities for you to practise your pop skills!

So, if you don't already know, all you have to do is take the first letter of the answer to each of the questions and unscramble the name to form another word or couple of words . . .

If you're a cheat, though, the answers are at the bottom of the opposite page!

B The name of a successful female solo artist . . .

1) Dreadlocks — a-go-go! This all-girl band had lots of hits — including 'Montego Bay' and 'Too Good To Be Forgotten' . . .

2) This kept up Lionel Ritchie and became a boogie classic . . .

3) A chart-topping series of double-compilation hit albums . . .

4) Like a flashback from 1972, this band arrived on the scene with an album called 'God's Own Medicine'.

5) A No. 1 hit in America for Simple Minds with this theme from 'The Breakfast Club'.

6) Paul Humphries and Andy McLuskey make up this wimpy Liverpool duo.

7) Phil Collins didn't feel the need for an overcoat when he released his second solo album . . .

C The name of a well-know hunky male solo singer . . .

1) 'Can I have The Pet Shop Boys album . . .?'

2) Prince's second film, shot in black and white on location in France . . .

3) If you wanted to get to know The Smiths, all you had to do was . . .

4) 'Welcome To The Pleasuredome' sold

46

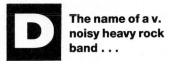

D — The name of a v. noisy heavy rock band . . .

1) This Dire Straits album was a best-seller worldwide and included 'Money For Nothing' and 'Walk Of Life' . . .

2) Frank Sinatra cashed in on an old hit when he returned to . . .

3) Lou Reed and a bunch of freaks were successful with 'Sunday Morning' and 'Venus In Furs' and called themselves . . .

4) Edwyn Collins wanted to 'Rip It Up' when he was frontman of . . .

5) Bob Geldof's autobiography asked . . .

6) This Simple Minds L.P. sounded like the beginning of a fairytale . . .

7) The cast of Grange Hill got together two years ago to record this anti-drugs song . . .

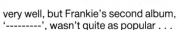

very well, but Frankie's second album, '---------', wasn't quite as popular . . .

5) Boys just wanna get noticed, but Cyndi Lauper says . . .

6) A tale of girls and engagements from those Wham boys . . .

7) A teethy American family band who were big in the 1970's . . .

8) No old tunes for Howard Jones — he first burst on to the scene with a . . .

9) The band that a not-so-fresh-faced Feargal Sharkey first appeared with . . .

E — The name of a famous T.V. pop show presenter . . .

1) What Vince Clarke and Alison Moyet called themselves when they teamed up to record 'Don't Go' and 'Only You' . . .

2) The song that accompanied A-ha's scribbly fantasy video . . .

3) Chrissie Hynde's band aren't for real . . .

4) Headbangers who 'Shook You All Night Long' on a 'Highway To Hell' . . .

5) Joe Strummer and The Clash explained that the big city was flooding with . . .

6) Swedish foursome who had big hits with 'Waterloo' and 'Name Of The Game' . . .

7) Sid, Johnny, Steve and Paul shocked the world as . . .

8) Martin Fry promised 'All Of My Heart' with . . .

9) Signing on with Ali and Robin Campbell . . .

10) His doctor might have been listening to Rod's chest with a stethoscope when Mr. Stewart charted this hit . . .

It's not a very nice feeling, but we've all been lonely at one time or another in our lives. Perhaps you've fallen out with a boyfriend and can't quite face going round with your old mates again, or perhaps you've moved house and don't know anyone in your new home town. Whatever the reason, it's definitely something everyone goes through, but it's the way you cope with it that tells most about you.

Do you start becoming bitchy and sarcastic, even although you don't mean to? Or do you make yourself into a doormat in an attempt to keep in with everyone, but end up friends with no-one? Those are two of the different ways loneliness can make you act. You can be so desperate to cover up your real feelings that what started off as a sort of play acting can take over — and you can't get out of the vicious circle.

Chances are you'll only recognise your own act. You'll think that everyone else is coping brilliantly while you're floundering desperately. This is because you're too wrapped up in your own loneliness to recognise the symptoms in anyone else.

We chatted to four Patches readers to see how they coped.

SARAH

Sarah is a nice girl who couldn't make friends because of her crippling shyness. Every time she tried to chat to someone, her shyness left her feeling as if she had nothing interesting to say. In an attempt to get people to notice and accept her, Sarah started making sharp, bitchy comments.

All right, you've got no sympathy at all for a girl like this. Girls like Sarah have probably hurt you once too often, even though you've tried to ignore them. But, if you think about it, bitchiness is just a defence mechanism. It's something to hide behind and usually the girl doesn't know how to come out of it.

Anyway, everyone uses bitchiness occasionally as a cover-up. You must have let slip the odd sneer when a boy you really liked walks past with a new girl. Turning that hurt you feel into a sarky remark comes easily, doesn't it? And girls like Sarah who get into the habit of sarky remarks end up having others hate them for it, and they become lonelier than ever.

Sarah didn't realise how much her viciousness had cost her, until a boy, Carl, started in her class. She was crazy about him from the start, like all the other girls. Then, at the end of his first week at school, his pen ran out just before the Maths lesson, and Sarah offered to lend him hers.

"He grinned at everyone," Sarah told us, "and shouted all round, 'Look, the Poison Dwarf's offering to lend me one of her poison pens!' Everyone fell about laughing.

And, unexpectedly, I burst into tears.

"I was surprised myself. I thought I'd got my act together and there I was, sobbing my socks off. It hit me, suddenly, how I'd ruined everything with my bitchiness. I didn't realise they called me The Poison Dwarf.

"But, when I started crying, everyone stopped laughing, and Carl said, 'Hey, listen, I didn't mean to upset you!' He sounded really concerned . That was the difference between him and me. He'd seen that other people have feelings, too, and he'd come right out and apologised when he'd said something to hurt me.

"So, that's what I'm trying to do now, just think about others a bit more. I'm trying to admit when I'm worried, or jealous, instead of sneering all the time, and one or two people have started talking to me again. Including Carl, incidentally."

So try not to fall into the trap of the quick sneer and the funny put-down just because you want to cover up your tears. It's not the way out!

MEL

It's difficult for a tomboy to adjust from playing football with the boys, climbing trees for conkers, being best mate of some local tearaway on a BMX, to realise that boys grow up and start looking at girls in a completely different way.

These girls have to try to recognise that their best friends, boys, are growing away from them. They can't bear the thought of becoming pathetic and simpering like the girls these boys now fancy.

Mel told us that she started throwing her weight around at school to compensate for the awkwardness she felt in

ONLY THE LONELY...

growing up and away from a group of older boys who had, when they were younger, always included her in their football games and bike rides. She hoped to impress them by proving that she was as tough as they used to be before they started taking girls out, and working for exams, and playing for school teams.

What she didn't realise was that one of the First Years she had tried to push around was the kid sister of one of her heroes. He grabbed her as she was swaggering out of school one day and accused her of bullying.

"So," Mel said, "I thought I'd show him! I said, 'What're you going to do about it, then?' sort of challenging him to fight it out, like little kids do. He just looked me up and down and said, 'Why don't you try to grow up, Mel? You used to be OK. I've reported you to the Head, that's what I've done', then he walked away.

"And the next day, I was in real trouble. Fortunately, the Head didn't send for my parents. She just talked to me, about growing up and coming to terms with it, and said I had a lot of good qualities, if only I'd use them. Then she put me on this Community Service option.

"I think that coming through that stage was a slow process. I had to stop trying to barge through life, and try to accept that my life was changing. I never was a real bully. I was just confused and unhappy."

You probably can't feel a lot of sympathy for what Mel did. She certainly hasn't any for herself! But try to feel some sympathy for why she behaved that way. Most girls go through this stage, and come out of the other side of it as pleasant as anyone else.

KERRY

At the other end of the scale is the doormat. Unhappily, she sits on the edges of all conversations, and is quite willing to do anything for anyone, just for a chance to get 'in' with the crowd.

Doormat is the one they send round to the chip shop. Doormat is the one who takes messages between a boy and the girl he fancies. Doormat shares her bag of crisps with everyone, and ends up with none left for herself. She's kind, considerate, never speaks unless she's invited to, and no-one gives her a second thought.

Kerry lives in Middlesborough. She's an only child and never had any real confidence in her ability to make friends. But she started spending her evenings in a local café where some of the girls from her school, and their boyfriends, used to meet. Because she's a willing and helpful girl, she didn't mind running after the girls she thought of as her 'friends'.

But none of these girls bothered with her in school, and one evening, upset because she'd overheard one of the girls say, "Isn't she a drag?!", she stayed away from the café. No-one noticed. No-one asked her where she'd been. No-one was interested.

"I think that's when I decided I'd been wasting my time with them. They weren't real friends. They'd been willing to use me, but I'd been willing to be used, hadn't I? I had no-one to blame but myself. Next day, I went out and joined this drama workshop that was starting up. I made myself do something for myself, instead of trying to force other people to share their lives with me."

If playing Doormat is your cover-up for loneliness, you've really got to rethink your act. You believe that if you do enough for others, they'll start to like you, and include you in their plans one day. Unfortunately, that's not strictly true.

What you have to start doing is to like yourself and then others will catch on.

So, no matter how lonely you feel, try saying, "No, I don't want to", or, "Don't push me around," occasionally. And when you're alone, try to think positively about yourself. Decide how great you really are. And let it shine through!

BEVERLEY

Some girls who've been through a recent heartbreak get it into their heads that because one romance went wrong, and one boy turned out to be a total swine, then no boys are worth bothering about, full stop.

Girls who appear to think this way can be a real drag. You can't rabbit on to them about this boy you fancy, because they'll just drone, "It's not worth it". When you burst in, all excited about what this boy said to you on Saturday night, and what you said back, and how he's asked you out on

Wednesday, they'll say, "Leave it alone. You'll only get hurt".

But this type of girl, drag or not, is the easiest to understand, because her hurt is so obvious. And, anyway, you've been there, haven't you? Everybody goes through the "I hate boys" stage at one time or another, but there's no point in letting it take over your entire life.

Beverley told us that she was devastated after her steady romance with Phil broke up. "It turned out he'd been two-timing me for weeks. I couldn't believe it. I thought he was perfect. And I'd worked so hard to keep him happy, and arrange things for the two of us to do together, because my last boyfriend had left me when he got involved with a Sunday soccer league. So Phil and I had a nice little routine going. And behind my back, on the nights he wasn't seeing me, he was seeing this other girl. He said he was doing a course in building maintenance for work, and I believed him!

"So, right off, I told all my mates to check up on where their boyfriends were, on the nights they weren't together. I went on and on about how you couldn't trust any boy. I thought I was giving them advice they'd welcome. But instead, they started avoiding me because I was such a misery.

"Then Jan, my best mate, said, 'Can't you see that if the romance isn't working, you're best out of it? And if it is working you have to get on and enjoy it! I'm actually enjoying going out with Gary. Do you remember what enjoying yourself felt like? Don't you want to be happy again, Bev?'

"She was the one who made me go to the school disco, and stop thinking that I'd be heartbroken for the rest of my life!"

What you have to realise, if you know that you're going on about how boys can't be trusted, is that far from covering up your loneliness, you're writing 'I'm upset' all over yourself in capital letters. Try to get the hurt into proportion.

You can try again. There *are* nice boys out there, and you're never going to get to meet one if you sit at home moping over a rat, are you? Anyway, why let that one boy ruin the rest of your life? If you think about it long enough you'll realise he really wasn't worth it — but there are plenty of other boys who are!

BUT I ONLY WANTED A TRIM...!

Not for the faint-hearted — but if you want to cause a stir, these are the styles to go for!

1. From Taylor Ferguson, 106 Bath Street, Glasgow.

2. Alan International, London.

3. Man's style (looks just as good on a girl) from Taylor Ferguson.

4. By Mason at Charlie Miller, Edinburgh.

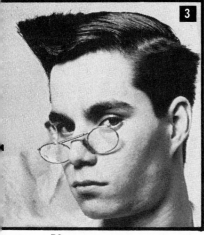

THROUGH THE BARRICADES

When Sharon Anderson refused to go out with me, I thought it was the end of the world. But when I met Kitty, I wondered what I had ever seen in Sharon . . .

"OK," she said suddenly. "We can see each other while I'm here."

IT was my brother Tom's fault that I went out that day at all.

"Stop moping around like a spoilt kid, Lee," he said impatiently. "I know Sharon gave you a knock back, but you're behaving like you only had three weeks to live. Get out of the house, go on. I'm sick of the sight of you."

Kind words indeed, I thought, as I pulled on my jacket and mooched out of the house. It was windy, and I pushed my hands deeper into my pockets. I couldn't stop thinking about last night at the disco.

"Now or never," my mate Jacko insisted, nodding to where Sharon was standing with Carol Lindsay and her boyfriend. I gulped. Sharon was looking pretty tasty. She's got this long frizzy blonde hair, and she was wearing a white mini skirt and white boots. I stood up deliberately and walked over to her.

"Hi, Lee," she'd said. All blue eyeliner and flowery perfume.

I shook myself awake. I didn't want to think about it anymore. To cut a long, embarrassing story short, I'd asked her to the pictures, and she'd said no.

A lot of noise and shouting made me look up. Further up the hill, on the wasteground near the quarry, there were crowds and crowds of people, loads of horseboxes and caravans.

"What the heck . . ." I muttered, but then I remembered. Each year at this time there was a horse fair, and gypsies and travellers from all over the country came to buy and sell animals. Curious, I decided to go up for a look. I like horses, providing they don't come any nearer than ten feet, and I'd nothing else to do anyway.

I ran up the hill and squeezed through to the front of the crowd. There was another crowd opposite, and a sort of road in between where people were running the horses up and down.

A tall, muscly guy was running up the path with a huge brown horse on the end of a rope. As it pounded past, I shrank back instinctively, but the man beside me craned forward for a better look.

"Fine-looking beast," he commented.

"Aye," agreed a voice behind him. "That's young Colley Merrick with it. He bought it here as a foal and brought it on himself. Did a grand job by all accounts."

The boy took the horse back up to the top, and the next one came down. It was a lean looking dark brown horse with black legs, not as big as the one

We liked the same music, the same films — all the corny things.

before, but twice as frisky.

"Nice youngster," said the man beside me to his friend. "Whose is that?"

"That belongs Merrick as well," the second voice said. "That's his young cousin with it. Keturah, her name is. Kitty."

It was then I noticed that the person with the horse was a young girl. She was small, dressed in jeans and wellies, and she had short brown hair. She kept her eyes on the ground but she happened to glance up as she was passing. I smiled at her, and her dark eyes lit up briefly.

When she had gone, I waited around for a few minutes, hoping she would come down again with another horse, but apparently that was Merrick's lot finished, so I pushed my way to the top end of the crowd to see if I could catch sight of her again. It was pretty hard to see anything through the mile thick wedge of horses milling around, but miraculously I caught sight of her disappearing into one of the little caravans. Oh well, that's the excitement over for today I thought as I made my way down the hill again. I was feeling a bit more cheerful now, at least. I didn't feel so bad about Sharon now that I'd seen there were other girls in the world after all.

Tom was pleased to see I'd cheered up when I got home. "Well, you're looking a bit more human now," he observed, as I raced him to the kitchen at teatime.

"Yeah. I took a walk up to the horsefair. It was quite good."

"What's her name?" Tom said casually.

"Kitty," I answered, a split second before I realised I'd been tricked. I grinned.

"You don't waste much time, little brother."

"She's a gypsy, Tom. I'll never be able to go out with her. She just made me realise that there is more to life than Sharon Anderson."

"OK, boys and girls," announced Mum as she cleared the table, "your dad and I are going out tonight, so I want one or two jobs done. I want the dishes washed and dried, the bin emptied, and someone can take Kim for a walk."

I was in no mood to empty bins or wash dishes, and I could tell from their faces that Tom and my sister Jane weren't either.

I made a grab for Kim's lead and I was out of the door faster than if someone had said Madonna was outside waiting for a date.

I took Kim down to the beach. It was windy and her black ears streamed behind her as she careered along the sand, scattering seaweed and terrifying seagulls. She's mental when she gets going. She won't stop for anyone or anything. I've known her run into walls before.

There were three people walking up ahead. A girl and two children. I could see Kim heading straight for them, and I imagined she'd no intention of stopping. I could just picture her manic grin, the tongue hanging out of her mouth and the fat paws flying. I started to run. "Kim! KIM! Come here!"

It was useless, of course. The wind was blowing in the wrong direction for one thing. Kim couldn't hear me, and the people ahead couldn't hear me. She smacked right into the back of the girl's legs and sent her sprawling in the sand. The children screamed with laughter.

"Flaming heck!" I muttered, running up to grab the dog. "Sorry," I said to the girl, who was laughing, "the dog's crazed."

"No problem," she said, and I looked up from putting Kim's lead on. It was Kitty.

I just stared, my mouth gaping open like a landed trout.

"Where have I seen you before?" she asked, curiously.

"At the sale this morning," I told her.

"That's right." She was pleased she'd remembered. "Do you like horses, then?"

"From a distance."

She smiled and we started to walk on. "How long are you here for?" I asked, screwing up my eyes against the flying sand.

"A fortnight. The fair only lasts a week, but a few of us are staying longer. Do you live here?"

"Yeah. My name's Lee. What's yours?"

"Keturah." She had a lovely accent. "Some people call me Kitty."

I decided to stick with Kitty. It was easier to remember, and the shortened form sounded more personal — well, I thought so, anyway.

We carried on walking and got deep into conversation. She told me that her parents were settled down, and that her father dealt in scrap metal.

"I'm here with my Auntie Thurzie and Uncle Kelly. They always bring a few horses, and my cousin usually needs a hand."

I remembered the guy with the horse.

We walked right along the beach, and I was head over heels by the time we got back. Kitty was great — small and dark, and she kept her two little cousins under control easily. She was so pretty — well, maybe pretty was the wrong word, but she was like no girl I'd fancied before. When we reached the foot of the hill by the quarry, she turned and grinned.

"Well, it was nice meeting you, Lee," Kitty said, with a quick, bright look at my face. "Maybe I'll see you again before we go."

Panic seized me. She wasn't getting away that easily. "Look — could we — I mean, can I see you while you're here? Go out now and again, I mean?"

Kitty seemed undecided. She looked up the hill after her cousins, who were running towards a tall dark boy — the other cousin, Colley, I supposed. He saw Kitty and waved.

"OK then," she said suddenly. "We can see each other while I'm here."

I couldn't believe it. "Great! What are you doing tonight?"

"Babysitting. But I'll tell you what, I have to do the shopping tomorrow, so I could meet you somewhere and you can show me where to go."

Tom and Jane thought it was hysterical that I was getting out of my pit to go shopping — during the holidays at that. "Serves you right for skiving off the washing up," Jane said smugly, but I was only too happy to get up at half past eight.

I met Kitty at the foot of the hill and took her into town.

It was the start of a brilliant fortnight. We met every day, and went for walks, or to the pictures, or into town. To begin with, I got a lot of slagging from the mates — "gypsy-lover", that type of thing. But once they got to know Kitty they thought the same as I did — that she was a great girl, good fun and always ready for a laugh.

But it was best when we were on our own. It seemed like we'd known each other for years. We liked the same music, the same films, we had the same sense of humour. All the corny things. I liked her more and more each time I saw her, and pretty soon she sensed that I was starting to get serious.

"Don't get too involved, Lee," she said once, concerned. "I'm only here for another week and then I won't see you again. I'm a traveller, Lee. It would never work."

I shrugged but said nothing. Personally, I reckoned she was being a bit dramatic, making a big fuss about nothing. She'd told me she lived with her parents, and they only stayed fifty miles away. It wasn't really that far — we could visit at weekends and holidays.

I imagined her teaching me to ride her old pony, meeting her parents, maybe even staying with her relatives. The only problem was, if I ever tried to talk to her about it, Kitty went all quiet and defensive. She refused to get involved, although she seemed to be enjoying herself OK the rest of the time. I learned not to talk about it if I didn't want the silent treatment.

"Look, Lee, let's just enjoy the time

"Don't get too involved, Lee," she said once.

we've got and take things as they come," she would say. Now who's behaving like they only had three days to live, I thought. I kept dropping hints and talking about holidays and bus fares and things but it seemed to annoy her.

Far from passing quickly, the fortnight seemed to last forever. Two days before she was due to leave, I decided it was about time we talked seriously about what we were going to do at weekends, and who would come to see who first.

"So what do you reckon? Could you draw me a map, or will you meet me at the station?"

When there was no answer, I looked up in surprise. Kitty's face was a mixture of anger, impatience and worry.

"Well?"

It was then she lost her temper. "Look, I told you, Lee! We can't see each other again. You have your life, I have mine, and I made that clear at the start! So leave off, will you!"

"What are you talking about?" I yelled back. "You're just dramatising as usual. OK, so you're a gypsy — big deal! You're settled down, aren't you? There's nothing to stop us seeing each other again if you'd stop being so awkward!"

"Why will you never accept things?" she screamed. "I can't see you again because I'm going to marry Colley!"

I felt as if someone had taken the heart right out of my body. *"What* did you say?" I asked, so quietly it was nearly a whisper.

Kitty drew a long shaky breath. "I'm going to marry Colley," she repeated, very quietly but very firmly. "It's been talked about for a long time."

"But he's your cousin," I said stupidly.

"No, he's my second cousin. Aunt Thursie's my mum's cousin."

"Then why —" I swallowed, trying to frame the words, "why did you agree to go out with me if you're engaged?"

"Oh, we're not engaged," Kitty said, her eyes on the ground. "But he's been taking me for granted recently, snapping at me, paying no attention to me. And I thought, well, if that's what he's like now, what's he going to be like when we're married? So when you asked me out, I thought I'd go, to give me and Colley a break from each other, and to see if it would bring him to his senses."

If I tried to talk to her, she went all quiet and defensive and wouldn't get involved.

"The last thing I wanted to do was hurt you, Lee . . ."

"You used me, in other words."

Kitty looked up, distressed. "*No —
well —* I suppose that's how it started.
But if you'd only accepted things for
what they were, instead of hassling me
all the time, you'd never have known.
The last thing I wanted to do was hurt
you, Lee . . ."

"Yeah," I said gruffly, "well it's a bit
late now."

She looked unhappy. "Well I'm sorry,
Lee. I really am. And if it's any
consolation, I'd have been happy to go
on seeing you if I was settled down. But
nothing would ever have come of it."

"How do you know?" I was curious in
spite of myself.

"Because you called me Kitty. I judge
people on what they call me, which
version of my name they prefer. And I've
found that people who call me Kitty can
very rarely understand me. I don't have
enough in common with them."

Running footsteps were heard and
we looked up simultaneously. Colley
was running down the hill towards us,
and he stopped halfway down when he
saw us looking. He stood there for a
minute, tall, broad, dark and his face was
unreadable.

"Keturah!"

I looked away. The use of her proper
name turned her into a completely
different person. It gave her new
dimensions, depth, it reflected her real
character. There couldn't have been
anything more personal than the way
Colley spoke her name.

"I'm coming." Kitty turned back to
me.

"Where are you going?"

"Don't know yet. I might see you next
year, though."

Next *year!* Next year was impossible.

"I'll write to you, Lee. But not often. It
wouldn't be fair to Colley."

I nodded. I couldn't really complain
— after all, I'd only asked her out to help
me forget about Sharon. It had worked.

Kitty looked up the hill. "I'll have to
go, Lee. I hope you'll be happy. Forget
about me and get on with your own life.
It's all you can do."

I nodded. "I hope you're happy too,
Kitty. Come and see me next year if
you're here."

She laughed. "Yeah, I might."

She turned and ran up the hill to
where Colley was waiting.

I didn't see Kitty again before she
left. I passed the next week in a sort of
stupor, and on the Friday I received a
letter postmarked Ayr.

"*. . . I had a great fortnight. It was
fun.*

"*It's great to be on the road again,
even if I am missing my parents. We're
up in Scotland for a while, but we're
having a bit of hassle about sites at the
moment, so we might be moving on
again soon.*

"*Colley and I are getting married in
the autumn. We're looking for a trailer of
our own just now, with the money he
made from the horses. Be happy for us!*

"*I hope things are going OK for you.
Take care and be happy,*

*Love
Kitty.*"

Kitty. She was Kitty for me, Keturah
for Colley. I had a part of her he couldn't
touch.

She was right. I had to put her behind
me and get interested in Sharon again.

Hopefully, it wouldn't be as difficult
as I thought. ■

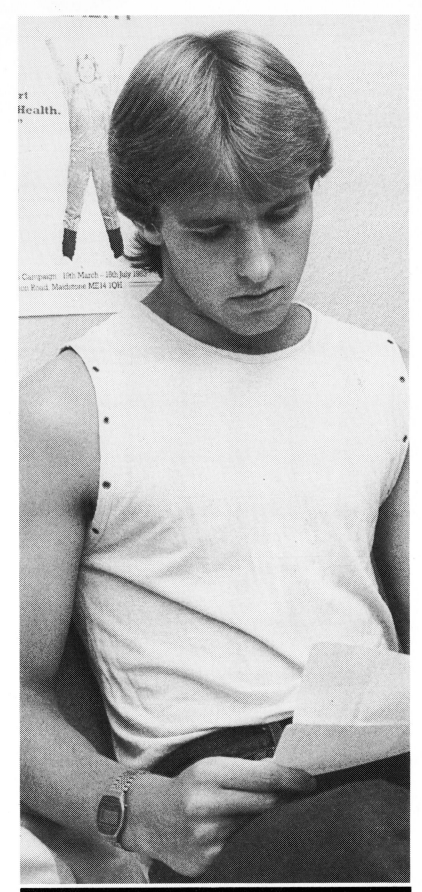

**". . . Colley and I are getting married in the
autumn . . ."**

If you talk to the trees, they'll come and take you away . . .! Despite rumours that they're suffering from the pressures of stardom, A-ha seem to be having a swinging time . . .

Digging in the dirt, Ozzy Osbourne emerges from a ditch to surprise us all with another of his rock comebacks . . .

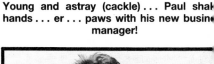

Surely meeting Mick Jagger, David Bowie and Daryl Hall must have gone to his head? Dave Stewart celebrates being king of the record producers by making up and wigging it a bit . . .

He used to slag off ageing hippies, but now, ageing punk Johnny Lydon is showing the wear and tear of the years and has a 'Rotten' taste in his mouth . . .!

LIGGIN', GIGGIN', AND POSIN'!

PATCHES' snappy photographers capture the stars on film, just when they least expect it!

Dedication's what you need . . . Susannah Hoffs of the Bangles didn't feel sleepy at all, so she decided to practice her karate *and* her guitar-playing at the same time!

At the road again . . . Michael J. Fox with his bag packed, heading off to Hollywood to start shooting another great movie . . .

Grunt and squeak and squawk with the animals . . . Madonna teaches her pet puma to scratch Sean Penn's ankles when he annoys her a bit too much . . .!

Pull the other one! Ben Watt of Everything But The Girl looking as if his face has just rung a bell . . .

Howard Jones licks his lips in anticipation of another bowlful of seaweed in tomato sauce . . .

"Who said I was thick? I can sign my name without looking *and* give you a silly grin at the same time!" Holly Johnson vandalising a few Frankie Goes To Hollywood album covers . . .

Wet knees ahoy! David Bowie enjoys playing in puddles, and doesn't care what his mum says . . .

LIGGIN', GIGGIN', AND POSIN'!

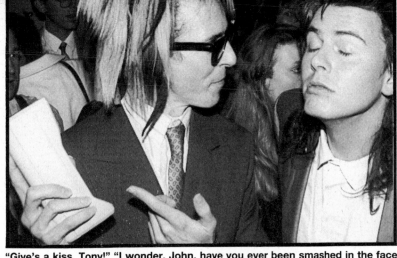

"Give's a kiss, Tony!" "I wonder, John, have you ever been smashed in the face with a hi-tech cordless battery-powered portable telephone!!"

"Gee! The service in this place is awful!" Hall and Oates, who're probably *still* waiting for their burgers . . .

Samantha Fox gets all frilly and looks for a push in the wrong direction . . . You'll never get your car started that way, dear!

Cast off on the rocks . . . Grace Jones, forgetting that one of the essential rules of sunbathing is to take off at least *some* of your clothes . . .!

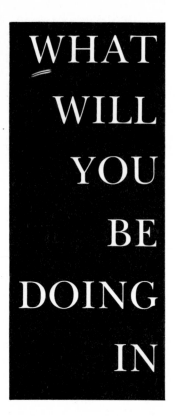

WHAT WILL YOU BE DOING IN TEN YEARS TIME?

WHAT will you be doing in ten years time?
You may be one of those lucky people who know exactly what they want to do when they leave school, but for most of us it can be a real problem finding a way to earn a living. If you're happy in your job it makes a big difference so you should choose a career that suits your personality and capabilities rather than aiming for the glamorous but impossible.

We've put together a few questions that should help to point you in the right direction.

1. You've got a cold and it's raining but you're determined to get to school because you've got a double period of which of the following subjects?
a) Maths or science,
b) Sports,
c) English or languages/drama, or
d) Art, needlework or cooking.

2. If you were a fly on the wall, how do you think people would describe you?
a) A friendly girl who's prepared to take on responsibilities,
b) A bundle of energy who's always on the go,
c) A real extrovert who always gets what she wants, or
d) Rather shy and reserved but well organised?

3. Saturday is yours to do whatever you want with. Which of the following activities would you be most likely to do?
a) You'd switch on the TV and flick through the latest mags and papers at the same time,
b) You'd go down to the youth club and rally some support for the charity walk next week,
c) You'd write a few letters, then tidy up your collection of Cliff Richard memorabilia, or
d) You'd go horse riding or swimming, or whatever sport you were into at the time.

4. Think carefully, which of the following *must* you get from a job?
a) Job satisfaction,
b) Masses of money and status,
c) Not a 9-5 job but one that involves your whole life, or
d) Security — you can't wait to sign up for the pension fund!

5. Close your eyes and imagine yourself in your ideal work setting. Which of the following is nearest your dreams?
a) You're behind the wheel of a flash car on your way to a meeting in the Big Smoke,
b) You're sitting in a plush office having a chat to one of your close friends and workmates,
c) You're just getting your coat on to go home when your bleeper goes and you're needed — there's an emergency, or

d) The rain's lashing down but you're happy because you've managed to find the lost lamb, and reunite it with its mother.

6. You may be stuck there for a while yet, so what's your real attitude to school?
a) You've got some good mates there, and, apart from the lessons, you manage to pass the time very constructively,
b) You can't wait to get out of the classroom, except when it's biology, and on to the sports field,
c) You find it all quite interesting especially now you're a prefect, or
d) You find some subjects a struggle but you do your best and take a pride in presenting what you do well.

Now check your answers to see if you scored mostly A's, B's, C's or D's, and then read on to discover the kind of job that would best suit you!

60

QUESTION ONE
a) D b) A c) B d) C

QUESTION TWO
a) D b) A c) B d) C

QUESTION THREE
a) B b) D c) C d) A

QUESTION FOUR
a) A b) B c) D d) C

QUESTION FIVE
a) B b) C c) D d) A

QUESTION SIX
a) B b) A c) D d) C

MOSTLY A'S

You're a lively sort, always on the move and keen to work outdoors. You'd never find any of the following jobs dull — sports centre staff, traffic warden, W.R.A.C., W.R.E.N., gardening assistant in a garden centre or grounds, sports teacher, groom, zoo assistant-keeper.

MOSTLY B'S

You're very confident and outgoing. If something's happening you're usually at the centre of things. Your lively, creative talents would be put to good use in the following occupations — journalist, actress, advertising executive, selling, public relations, T.V., film and radio.

MOSTLY C'S

You enjoy your own company, are thoughtful and well-organised. However, you don't really have the confidence to make big decisions and would therefore probably prefer not to be your own boss. Some of the following jobs may suit you — typist, secretary, librarian, clerk, researcher, draughtsperson.

MOSTLY D'S

You take life seriously and you're very responsible so you'd feel you were doing something worthwhile if you were involved in any of the following occupations — nursing, social work, catering, receptionist and telephone switchboard jobs, radiographer, medicine, lab assistant, chemist.

61

About to go to college or university? Bet you're dying to get started — but a bit scared too! So, read on for a few tips on how to get through that all–important first year!

Making the decision to carry on in full-time education after you've left school is becoming more and more an attractive option because of the lack of jobs available for the unqualified. There's no doubt that you stand a better chance of a job if you have a degree or a certificate or diploma from a polytechnic under your belt. But having been accepted for a place, you need to have your wits about you if you're to stay the course. We spoke to a few students and they were happy to pass on some tips for freshers!

SO YOU'VE LEFT HOME. NOW WHAT?

Being accepted for a place in a college in another town will mean leaving home — often for the first time. That may sound great — all that freedom — no Mum and Dad to check up on you, insist you're in at a reasonable time, and nag at you for not tidying your room.

But there's the other side to consider. What happens when you're stuck on the wrong side of town after a late party — and there's no Dad on the other end of a phone to taxi you home?

Late nights mean late mornings — and no Mum to waken you with a cup of coffee. And if you don't tidy up your room after you, no-one else will! Which is OK until you have to rummage under a pile of clothes, frantically searching for a clean bra!

There are advantages and disadvantages obviously, but the main thing to remember is that you're responsible for yourself. If you want to live like a slob, miss lectures and stay out all night — that's fine, as long as you realise you'll probably fail all your exams, get a bad reputation and end up flat broke!

The thought of moving into a flat with another couple of girls may be appealing, but if you're not used to sharing, doing chores, or cooking it could be a disaster for everyone. As Anne says; "I was never fanatically tidy at home, but I did clear up at least once a week. When I moved into a flat with three other girls I couldn't believe the mess! And you could never get into the bathroom — it was hopeless!"

Halls of Residence may be more restrictive, but they will break you in gently to life away from home. And once you feel you can cope, then you can think about getting a flat and becoming more independent.

Another problem you may not have

considered is homesickness. It can hit you like a ton of bricks — but don't worry — it will almost certainly pass.

You don't have to stick it out alone, though. All colleges and universities have guidance counsellors who are there to talk over your problems and offer advice.

HERE COMES COLLEGE

YOU DON'T HAVE TO BE LONELY

One of the problems about starting a new life in a new place is that you seem to be the only person in the entire universe who doesn't know anyone. But the solution isn't to sit in your room night after night reading your 'Sociology For Beginners'and wondering why everyone's at a party except you.

Colleges and universities *are* for working hard, but they're also for having a certain amount of fun, too. And one glance at a typical college notice board will tell you that there's something for everyone to do, and to join.

So grit your teeth, take a deep breath and go for it.

If you can't find anything that interests you, put your own notice up. There may be hundreds of other upside-down roller skaters just dying to meet you!

Don't, on the other hand, go around joining everything in sight. Remember the main reason you're there — to get that degree or certificate, so leave enough time for work.

But take time off to enjoy yourself sometimes and you'll find you work better because of, rather than in spite of, it.

BUT YOU DO HAVE TO WORK

You'll find — perhaps to your great delight at first — that university or college is very different from school. No-one will bother much if you miss lectures or you're late with essays. This may sound wonderful, but then again it means you have total responsibility for how much work you do.

As Susan (19) says, "In my first year I was having such a great time — going to parties and discos. I kept missing early lectures, then I'd think, well, no point in going for half a day . . . By Christmas I was so far behind I had to miss all the fun and work through the night to have a chance of passing the term exams."

It sounds boring, but it's far easier to work steadily doing a little each night, than none at all and then cramming it all in a week before your exams — you'll only get totally confused and fail miserably.

Having trouble keeping up is a different matter. Lecturers aren't unapproachable and they have more time than teachers, so if you're having trouble, ask for extra tuition and you'll find they'll be glad to help.

BOYS . . . BOYS . . . BOYS . . .

. . . . as far as the eye can see — wall to wall, in fact! Of course they only make up around 50% of the population, but when you arrive in your new environment it may seem as if they're coming out of the woodwork!

Don't worry — the population hasn't changed in favour of girls — it's just that you're in an enclosed environment and all these male faces are new to you. The ones back home are so familiar you just don't notice them anymore.

It's the same for them — and you may find you could be out with a different guy every night — 'terrific!', you may think — and you're probably right — but here's a word of warning from Andrea (18). "Before I left home, I'd only been out with three or four guys — I'm quite shy really. But when I got here it was great — I could forget myself — no-one knew me and I pretended to be a real party girl.

"But it soon caught up with me. I got tired of the empty compliments, endless one night stands and never really getting to know anyone. I've got a steady guy now and I'm much happier — and I get better marks!"

Take Andrea's advice and don't accept every invitation you get — you've got three or four years to get round them all!

MAKING FRIENDS

Meeting new people with different ideas can be a really exciting feeling — you want to be like them, experiment with all the things they do, be a part of their exclusive scene. But be wary . . . Jim (18) "In the small town where I come from I'd never even heard the names of half of the drugs people talked about at university. So when I was offered some I didn't want to seem like a country boy with no experience of drugs — which is exactly what I was! Luckily that one experience put me right off, but it's all too easy to be persuaded into doing something you'll really regret. My advice is the same as the Grange Hill Mob — just say no."

Away from home, a whole new world opens up — some experiences will be enjoyable — others won't. But try to learn by your mistakes — and don't make the same ones twice.

MONEY — AND THE LACK OF IT

A student grant can seem like a fortune if you're fresh out of school and have only had pocket money or a few pounds earned from a part-time job before. But it has to go a long way! You need to budget if you're to make each term's grant cheque last out.

Banks are willing to help and most issue special booklets with advice on budgeting, details of bank charges, overdraft facilities and often a gift of book vouchers or something similar to encourage you to use their bank. None of this is warm-hearted on their part, however — they charge you for all their services and will soon be after your blood if you overdraw constantly.

Once you've selected a bank, deposited your first term's grant cheque and worked out a budget, take out a set amount of money each week and try to stick to that. Obviously, some weeks unexpected expenses arise, but if you've budgeted carefully you should be back to normal in a couple of weeks. Budget sense learned now will stand you in good stead in the future when you get a job and wage packet!

The best way to deal with offers of credit cards which urge you to buy now and pay later is — forget it! A student grant does not support impulse buys — which are exactly what retail store charge cards encourage you to do. You'll end up in debt, worried and very unhappy.

So until you have a job, just forget it. If you can't pay cash, don't buy it.

So, all that remains is for you to pack your suitcase (remember your toothbrush) and go!

THE NAME GAME!

How can numbers tell you anything about your personality?

You might think they can't, but that's where you'd be wrong, isn't it, nerdy!

Printed below is a Numerology chart called the "Hewbrew System". Each letter of the alphabet corresponds to a number, and all you do is write down your full name, put the corresponding number under each letter, then total it up. Easy, eh? The only thing is, it has to come to a number between one and nine — but don't panic! If your number is 15, just add 1 + 5 — and your number is 6!

If the numbers in your name add up to ONE then you, like Madonna, are heading for the top in whatever field you choose! No. 1 people are ambitious, forceful individuals with strong qualities of leadership. But, although they may be highly successful, they get there by sheer hard work and determination. They like to dominate and need to be admired, but in spite of their outward confidence they often feel isolated and lonely. It isn't easy for them to make friends. They're sometimes too busy making money!!!

If 2 is your name number you're much less ambitious than a 1 person, but you're very loyal and conscientious. Content to be a follower, not a leader, you can still get your own way — but with gentle persuasion. You're very shrewd and your mates will often come to you for advice. You're inclined to be a bit moody, though, so guard against being a miseryguts when everything isn't going your way!

No. 3 folk are outgoing, sociable and you'd never miss them in a crowd! Like 1 they're also destined for success, and they're usually so big-headed they wouldn't settle for anything less! They have tons of energy, drive and enthusiasm. But their tendency to become easily bored and restless means they can't concentrate long on one topic before flitting to another. So a lot of their boundless energy is scattered and wasted!

4, like 2, is reliable and hardworking. So if you're a 4, you're stable and practical with sound judgement and commonsense. Just in case you're worried that this all sounds as if you're a boring swot, you can add a streak of rebelliousness and stubborness, and a pretty explosive temper which can really surprise people who don't know you very well. 4's have to work hard for everything they get, but no matter how many disappointments hit them, they always bounce back.

5 is quick thinking, clever and creative! No. 5 people are highly strung, sensual individuals, often physically attractive, with varied, but sometimes troublesome love lives! Their demand for personal freedom is the cause of a lot of strained relationships where boys are concerned, but funnily enough, they're the easiest number to make friends with! They're extrovert, outspoken and imaginative, and if you're a 5 and you fancy a creative sort of job either in the artistic or writing field, it looks like you're on a winner!

If you're 6 you're very lucky, for this is supposed to be the perfect number for peace, balance and harmony! You're warm, caring and emotional and, being an avid fighter for those worse off than yourself, are often drawn into "caring professions" like nursing. 6 people love their homes and families, and are certainly the happiest and most fulfilled of all numbers.

The number 7 has always had an air of mystery about it. It has religious and biblical associations, but 7 people are also often intrigued by the supernatural and love to read a good horror story! Sevens can be loners at times but they're quite happy with their own company. You'll be pleased to know that 7's traditionally a lucky number, and 7 folk can expect plenty of travel and excitement in their future.

8 is the money number! If you're an 8, you'll be successful, but more in the world of high finance and big business than art or entertainment. If you're No. 8 it's likely your friends will find you somewhat aloof and difficult to understand. You're not really as snooty as you seem — you're scared to unwind too much as you're afraid of being hurt. Anyone who does get to know you well will find a heart of gold and a great sense of humour.

Number 9 is a real romantic — caring, compassionate and creative. They tend to concern themselves with fighting for 'causes' and people who are deprived. They're often argumentative and stubborn, but in their favour it must be said that their arguments are usually sound! They're always ready with an understanding, sympathetic ear!

1	2	3	4	5	6	7	8
A	B	C	D	E	U	O	F
I	K	G	M	H	V	Z	P
Q	R	L	T	N	W		
J		S			X		
Y							

for example:

```
M A D O N N A     L O U I S E
4 1 4 7 5 5 1     3 7 6 1 3 5

V E R O N I C A   C I C C O N E
6 5 2 7 5 1 3 1   3 1 3 3 7 5 5
```

● Added together these numbers total 109. Then because you don't have a single digit you add 1+0+9=10 and 1+0 = 1. So 1 is Madonna's number!

Try it with your own name, and see what type of person you are.

GHOSTBUSTERS!

It was Friday night at the youth club . . .

I DON'T CARE WHAT ANYBODY SAYS. I WOULDN'T BE CAUGHT DEAD IN A GRAVEYARD!

AW, COME ON, JANE. IT'LL BE A LAUGH.

WHAT'S EVERYBODY TALKING ABOUT?

HI, ALISON. WE'RE HAVING A DISCUSSION ABOUT GHOSTS.

GHOSTS?

YEAH, CAROL WATCHED A VIDEO OF 'POLTERGEIST 2' LAST NIGHT, AND IT STARTED US TALKING ABOUT SPOOKY THINGS.

ANDREW'S DEAD INTELLIGENT. HE MUST BE, 'COS HALF THE TIME I DON'T KNOW WHAT HE'S TALKING ABOUT!

I DON'T KNOW HOW ANYBODY CAN BELIEVE THAT STUFF. IT'S ALL A LOAD OF RUBBISH. WHEN PEOPLE THINK THEY'VE SEEN A GHOST, ALL THEY'VE REALLY WITNESSED IS A MANIFESTATION OF PSYCHIC ENERGY IN THE ATMOSPHERE.

I REALLY FANCY HIM, THOUGH. I WISH THERE WAS SOME WAY I COULD GET HIM INTERESTED IN ME . . .

At that moment, though, he seemed more interested in ghosts . . .

THE OLD GRAVEYARD?

YOU WEREN'T SERIOUS ABOUT THAT, WERE YOU? IT'LL BE A WASTE OF TIME!

YOU CAN'T JUST DISMISS IT LIKE THAT, ANDREW. NOBODY CAN BE SURE IF GHOSTS EXIST OR NOT. THAT'S WHY I THINK WE SHOULD ALL GO TO THE OLD GRAVEYARD TOMORROW NIGHT, AND SEE WHAT HAPPENS.

WHAT AN EYE-OPENER!

Come on, all you spectacle

wearers out there! It's time to

come out of the closet and

get yourself noticed with

these great fashion frames . . .

Available from branches of leading opticians.

Our thanks to staff of Dolland and Aitchison for their help.

THAT'S WHAT WE WERE TALKING ABOUT BEFORE YOU CAME IN. THERE'S A RUMOUR AROUND TOWN THAT THE LOCAL GRAVEYARD'S HAUNTED. WE'RE THINKING OF SPENDING TOMORROW NIGHT THERE, TO SEE IF THE GHOST SHOWS UP!

NOT ME. I'D BE SCARED STIFF! HANGING ABOUT A GRAVEYARD IN THE MIDDLE OF THE NIGHT ISN'T MY IDEA OF FUN.

OK THEN. I STILL SAY IT'LL BE A WASTE OF TIME —BUT WE'LL ALL MEET IN THE GRAVEYARD AT MIDNIGHT TOMORROW.

OH . . . ANDREW'S GOING. I DIDN'T THINK HE WOULD BE . . .

So . . .

I'LL BE EVER SO SCARED IN THAT CREEPY GRAVEYARD, ANDREW. WILL YOU PROTECT ME IF THE GHOST SHOWS UP?

YOU WON'T NEED PROTECTING. I KEEP TELLING EVERYBODY, THERE'RE NO SUCH THINGS AS GHOSTS!

THOUGHT YOU SAID YOU WEREN'T COMING, ALISON? IT DIDN'T TAKE YOU LONG TO CHANGE YOUR MIND!

I JUST DECIDED IT MIGHT BE FUN, AFTER ALL.

I'LL BET I CAN GUESS WHY. SHE'D GO ANYWHERE ANDREW GOES, JUST TO TRY TO GET HIM TO NOTICE HER . . .

WHAT DOES ALISON SEE IN THE GUY? HE'S NOTHING BUT A BIG-HEADED SHOW-OFF.

BESIDES, THERE ARE PLENTY OF FAR NICER, BETTER-LOOKING BLOKES THAN HIM WHO'D JUST LOVE TO TAKE HER OUT . . . ME, FOR INSTANCE . . .

On Saturday afternoon . . .

I DON'T SUPPOSE I'LL GET MUCH CHANCE TO TALK TO ALISON TONIGHT. SHE'LL BE HANGING ROUND ANDREW ALL THE TIME.

I'M SURPRISED HE EVEN DECIDED TO COME. I DON'T KNOW WHY HE'S BOTHERING, WHEN HE THINKS IT'S ALL SUCH A WASTE OF TIME . . .

Then . . .

THAT CROWD AT THE YOUTH CLUB ARE A RIGHT LOAD OF WALLIES. THEY REALLY THINK THEY MIGHT SEE A GHOST TONIGHT!

THAT'S ANDREW'S VOICE. HE MUST BE WITH ONE OF HIS MATES FROM COLLEGE . . .

At midnight . . .

Andrew was getting changed, too . . .

THE END

Horsin' Around

Lots of people think horse-riding is snobby or just for the rich, while others think all you do is sit on the horse and kick! But there's a lot more to horse-riding than that. Done properly, it's great exercise (you'll use almost every muscle in your body), very challenging, exciting and lots of fun!

Learning To Ride

LEARNING to ride is fairly cheap for what you get and it's a lot of fun.

The most important thing is to make sure you use a riding school which is approved by the British Horse Society. That way you'll know you're being taught properly by a qualified instructor and that the horses are healthy and well-looked after.

Any school which has an untidy yard and horses wearing dirty saddles and bridles should be avoided. It won't be a safe place to learn.

It's best to make your first few lessons private ones, so that the instructor is paying attention to you and not trying to watch a whole class at once. You'll probably start learning with your horse on a lunge rein — a long rein which runs from your horse's noseband to the instructor's hand. This way, you can concentrate on your position in the saddle without having to worry about controlling the horse, too.

You should wear boots or shoes with heels to stop your feet slipping through the stirrups and a hard hat, which you'll be able to hire from the riding school.

Lots of people think horse-riding's an expensive sport but when you add up the instructor's wages, the cost of feeding, shoeing and equipping the horse as well as the use of the land and buildings, an hour's riding at about £7.00 is pretty cheap!

Holidays

HORSEY holidays are brilliant — especially if you go with a lot of friends. Less experienced riders should choose a trekking holiday. The pace is usually pretty slow — the aim is to relax and enjoy the scenery, so the ponies will be safe and steady.

If you're pretty experienced and fancy something more exciting, a trail-riding holiday is the thing for you. They usually include lots of fast work across country and you'll probably spend nights at inns or farmhouse lodgings so you can travel further afield.

If you're pretty serious about your riding, though, and want to learn as well as have fun on your holiday, a visit to a good equestrian centre would be the best idea.

During your stay there, you'll usually have a chance to hack out, have lessons, learn more about caring for horses and maybe even enter a show.

You'll find lots of adverts for horsey holidays in any equestrian magazine.

It's best to choose a centre which is approved by the British Horse Society.

Continued from previous page

Working With Horses

WORKING with horses means dirt, hard work, dedication and a practically non-existent social life, so make sure it's what you really want before you take up a career with horses.

Groom

WORKING as a groom involves lots of hard work — mucking out, grooming, feeding, cleaning the yard — but this is how nearly everyone involved with horses starts out.

Lots of people find they like the job and won't move on, except perhaps to different establishments, while others will be using grooming as a stepping stone to become a riding instructor.

If you want to make this your career, you should consider the Association of British Riding Schools Grooms Diploma.

Candidates should be 18 or over with at least 18 months full-time work experience with horses. The exam covers subjects such as stable management, riding, feeding, lungeing and veterinary matters.

Riding Instructor

OF all horsey jobs, this is usually the best paid and good instructors are always in demand.

You should get as much experience of horse management and riding as you can and then sit the British Horse Society's Assistant Instructors Certificate. You need a very good all-round knowledge of horses, you must be a good rider and be able to teach someone else.

The next step is the Intermediate Instructors Certificate and then the Instructors Certificate.

Most people train for these exams as a working pupil — working in return for tuition, although it is possible to pay and complete the course in a shorter time.

Everyone has to pay to sit the exam.

Useful Addresses

The British Racing School, Snailwell Road, Newmarket, Suffolk.

British Horse Society, National Equestrian Centre, Stoneleigh, Warwickshire, CV8 2LR.

Association of British Riding Schools, 44 Market Jew St., Penzance, Cornwall, TR18 2HY.

Showing

THIS is really just showing off the pony to its best advantage. There are in-hand classes, where the ponies aren't ridden, usually because they're too young, and there are the ridden classes.

The ponies are divided into three sections according to their height — 12.2 hands and under, 13.2 hands and under, and 14.2 hands and under. They must be well turned out, with clean tack and plaited manes, and the rider must be immaculate too.

All that's involved is that the ponies walk, trot and canter round the ring, then, once the judge has had a look at them, they're called into line in order.

Each pony will have to do an individual show, and occasionally the judge will ask for the saddle to be removed and the pony to be run out in hand.

Then the class walk round the ring again and are called in in their final line-up.

The judge is looking for a well-turned out pony and rider, and expects the pony to be well-schooled and obedient. The result of the class is very much down to the judge's personal taste, and a pony's placing will probably vary considerably with different judges.

Eventing

NO doubt you've heard of three-day-eventing, but as a rule, this is only for the big shots. However, riding clubs all over the country hold one day events which are more or less the same thing, but on a much simpler scale.

Again, ponies go according to height. The first section of the competition is a dressage test which the rider will have learned beforehand and is now expected to perform from memory. There isn't anything too complicated involved, and you'll be judged on each movement.

The next section is the cross-country phase. This consists of riding a course of jumps built to look as much like natural obstacles as possible. Cross country takes a lot of courage and stamina. There will be a lot of mud, ditches and probably one or two water jumps, so if you don't like getting dirty, avoid cross-country at all costs!

The final phase is a round of showjumping.

All your scores, times and faults are taken into consideration and the pony who has done best overall wins.

A good eventing pony is very special. He has to be quiet and collected for the dressage phase, bold and fast for cross-country, and balanced and steady for showjumping.

A one-day-event is great fun if a bit exhausting. If your pony doesn't do well in the dressage, he might make it up in the cross-country.

You can learn a lot taking part in a one day event!

Dressage

DRESSAGE really means to train a horse to be supple and totally obedient to the rider's commands.

It might sound simple but is actually very difficult as the horse is taught to perform movements it would never do without a rider and to train a top dressage horse can take seven years.

In the simplest tests, you'll probably only be asked to walk, trot and canter on each rein with a couple of halts in between, but as you progress, the tests will be become more and more complicated.

To become a good dressage rider, you'll need lots of practice and help from an experienced teacher.

Horsey Happenings

THERE are lots of horsey events going on all round the country, especially in summer.

Check the local press for details of shows in your area — The Pony Club, riding clubs and even local riding schools will hold their own shows which you can watch.

County shows are well worth a visit. The standard is usually high and if you live in Scotland make an effort to visit The Royal Highland Show at Ingliston near Edinburgh.

Badminton is the eventers' event of the year, where you can see all the top riders competing. It's held in the spring, with the first two days devoted to dressage, third to cross-country and the fourth to showjumping.

But for glamour and a sense of occasion, you can't beat the spectacular Horse of The Year Show at Wembley.

You'll see all the top showjumpers there, as well as champion show ponies from all over the country, displays, police horses, driving, heavy horses and Pony Club mounted games — even people who're not that keen on horses will enjoy the thrills and spills!

It's traditionally held the first full week of October and tickets are available from the Wembley Arena Box Office.

Before

To The Rescue

JUST like other animals, some horses, ponies and donkeys are treated very badly — beaten, starved or just abandoned to fend for themselves.

The lucky ones end up in horse sanctuaries like Redwings.

Wendy Valentine, who founded Redwings Horse Sanctuary nearly five years ago, now has 180 horses, ponies and donkeys in her care.

SOME of the animals were saved from slaughter, some rescued from sales, others from private owners who didn't know how to look after them.

"The main problem," Wendy told us, "is people who don't know the first thing about horses but decide to buy one. Usually, they've got a horse-mad child and they just don't realise what's involved in keeping a horse or pony."

Horse sanctuaries raise money in lots of ways. Redwings have an adoption scheme where you pay a few pounds each year in return for newsletters and information on your chosen pony.

They also market a range of gifts and are open to the public every Sunday (2.00-5.00) from Easter until Christmas. The gift shop is open and there are pony rides and a tombola as well as the chance to see the rescued animals.

If you'd like to send a donation or receive information on the adoption scheme or anything else concerning the sanctuary, write to: The Secretary, Redwings Horse Sanctuary, Hill Top Farm, Hall Lane, Frettenham, Nr. Norwich, Norfolk.

Showjumping

THIS is about riding a pony round a course of roughly ten coloured fences. There will be a variety of jumps to contend with — spreads, doubles, and sometimes even combinations. You have to be alert and in control all the time, judging turns and distance and timing.

For a knock-down you get four faults, and for a first refusal three faults. The second refusal counts as six faults, and a third results in elimination.

There are all different sorts of showjumping classes. Ponies are again divided into sections by their height, but other classes include the Scurry, where you must complete your round as fast as possible, the Take-Your-Own-Line where you choose your own course over the fences, and the Chase-Me-Charlie, where all the ponies jump one after the other over a fence which is raised higher and higher until there's one winner.

A lot of places hold shows in their indoor schools which means you can compete all winter too.

Showjumping is harder than it looks, but it's a lot of fun — if your pony enjoys it. If he doesn't, it'll be more trouble than it's worth to compete!

After

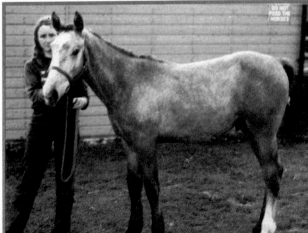

You're at the

party of the year,

decked out like a

dog's dinner,

when all of a

sudden, you spot

the dog — the

boy who makes

you want to —

THE MUSIC BUFF

THE FASHION VICTIM

THE MUSIC BUFF

How to spot him

The first sign is usually an eyeful of tour dates. His back will be facing you, and his head buried in a heap of records in front of the stereo. You won't know for at least an hour what his face actually looks like (he's organising the "sounds" you see!), but you'll be able to recite the exact progress of David Bowie's 1978 tour of Inner Mongolia off by heart!

How to avoid him

Stand perfectly still — do not dance, do not sing, do not pass GO, do not collect £200! DO NOT MOVE A MUSCLE! As soon as he sees you're really getting into the groove, he'll be across faster than you can say U2!

His ideal partner

Someone who can find him the original 12" remix dance version of Simple Minds' cover version of the Greek National Anthem (sung in Portuguese, of course . . .).

THE FASHION VICTIM

How to spot him

You'll have to have your wits about you to spot this one. He'll be skulking away in a corner trying to protect his jacket from the ravages of the party-goers. He's not actually there to enjoy himself, just to show off his new gear.

He may occasionally venture out to study the cut of someone's jacket, or the texture of a tie, but his only conversation will sound like a mail order catalogue on tape.

You'll end up thinking Flip and Liberty are good friends of his.

How to avoid him

If you see him heading in your direction, dash to the nearest wardrobe, find a pair of puce wellies, a paisley patterned balaclava, and a duffel coat preferably covered in cat fluff. Just be careful, though, that it's not what they're all wearing in Paris next spring!

His ideal partner

Well, he's been trying to contact Miss Selfridge for years!

PICK UP YOUR

THE FOOD FIEND

THE SOCIAL CLIMBER

THE LADY KILLER

How to spot him
If you decide to make for the buffet, he's sure to be there! Clutching his Donald Duck paper plate and his Mr Man plastic cup, he'll survey the buffet like a lion waiting for the moment to pounce on his prey — then he'll move in for the kill of four sausage rolls, half a ton of crisps, a hot dog or seven, and perhaps a smidgeon of side salad.

But then he'll want to discuss at length the value of what he's eaten and how it compares to other party nosh he's tried. The flakiness of the pastry, the spice content of the punch. You'll find yourself becoming less and less hungry . . .

How to avoid him
Diet!

His ideal partner
Unless you cook like Delia Smith or own shares in Sainsbury's, I'm afraid you don't stand much of a chance — which can only be a good thing!

How to spot him
Standing alone, looking outrageously bored, asking where all the photographers are. He'll wander around aimlessly, tapping people on the shoulder saying, "Dahling, I haven't seen you since . . . it must have been George's do at the Hippodrome. Soopah, wasn't it?"

Of course the poor unsuspecting female will look totally bewildered and turn away unimpressed. Nothing daunts him however, and after a few tales of trendy encounters he'll be off looking for likely reporters to the gossip columns.

How to avoid him
When he taps you on the shoulder, hoping you're Lady Helen Windsor visiting distant relatives, turn around and say, "Should I know you?" It'll kill him!

His ideal partner
Anyone remotely famous. If you're not remotely famous — find someone who's more interested in chips than champagne.

How to spot him
You'll hear him before you see him, he'll be there, breathing down your neck and it will be a while before you actually pluck up the courage to turn around!

When you do, watch yourself — this lot usually have the looks to back up their chat, but in their back pocket have a calculator just in case they lose count of their conquests.

How to avoid him
Ask for his calculator, add one to his present total and while he's congratulating himself, make yourself scarce . . .

His ideal girl
Not many qualifications needed here — be female and be warned!

PATCHES SAYS IN ALL THESE CASES — HIDE YOURSELF!

OAT AND RUN!

Second Time Around!

Making ends meet isn't an easy task, and buying clothes can be a pauper's nightmare. It's a good idea then, to acquaint yourself with the great art of jumbling. It's a myth that you have to have a pension book and a sharp straw basket for poking other people out of the way in order to qualify for this pastime. The following is a guide to successful jumbling . . .

The venue _____
Scour the local paper for Friday night hotspots, such as church halls and Scout huts where jumble sales, or their upmarket equivalent, jamborees, are being held. Get yourself and your mates (this is not a solitary sport) there early to beat the crowds.

The equipment _____
A pocketful of jangling change is a must, as are numerous poly bags for storing your finds. Don't take handbags or other dangly bits, for if you put anything down for a minute to gather your strength, you could find your customised leather jacket has been sold for ten pence to a lady who wants to chop it up for window cloths.

The rules

The first hurdle is getting anywhere near the clothes stalls. It can be a tense moment when you realise that if you don't get in soon, all that'll be left are the bobbly jumpers and well-stretched jeans you gave to the little scout when he came round last week. You must summon up all your courage and squeeze yourself into the writhing throng, where clothes are being passed hand-over-fist. You have to be quick here as failure to grab your chosen garment the minute it catches your eye could result in it being propelled up the stall to disappear forever amongst the white elephants.

It does no good to politely ask the woman seven bodies up in the queue to pass you the "perfectly preserved Edwardian tea-dress", because if you're even heard above the clamour, a swarm of antique dealers will descend like crows upon said tea-dress, and in the ensuing riot you'll be blamed for causing a breach of the peace.

This line could be a good wheeze, though, if you want the other end of the stall to yourself.

The prizes

It's no good grabbing slightly out-of-date jackets or court shoes with broken heels. When you get that lot home, you'll only wonder why you bought carbon copies of everything in your wardrobe you don't particularly like.

It's a fact of life that you have to face, you're unlikely to come across leggings and jumpers in this season's colours, so you have to exercise your imagination as well as your muscles if you're going to come out of the Scout hut with a new wardrobe.

What you might find are real ski-pants, cotton print dresses and skirts, fifties suits, flappy overcoats, dustercoats, fitted blouses, baggy shirts, Crombies, cashmere cardies, suede jackets ... yes, the list is endless.

The main thing to remember is that if something only costs you a few pennies you can risk messing it up in an attempt to alter it. Big dresses can be cut into skirts or just belted for a casual look. Grubby, but otherwise perfect blouses can be washed in a solution of bleach to make them white again, or dyed to go with something else. (Read the instructions on the bottles and tins carefully though.)

Fancier stuff like cocktail dresses and evening suits can crop up, but if you're not the sort to wear them, there's not much point in crowding out your wardrobe with dead foxes and maribou feathers. (Here speaks the voice of bitter experience, *and* it makes you feel guilty every time you open the wardrobe to two beady, reproachful little eyes.)

It's also worth having a look round the other stalls for accessories. Hats, bags, gloves, brooches, beads, earrings, scarves, all help to make an outfit look complete, or brighten up something dull.

When you get it all home, you need to wash and iron the clothes, repairing any rips or broken zips. What makes jumbling clothes look tatty is lack of care, not the fact that they're secondhand.

So, next time you're stuck for something to do on a Saturday morning, other than window shopping, clear a space in your wardrobe and head for the jumblies!

"I WANNA BE IN PICTURES!"

If you've ever wondered what goes on behind the scenes in our photographic sessions — take a look into the life of James Jordan, one of our favourite photographers . . .

Monday 9 a.m., the Fashion Ed. phones James.

YOU WANT TO DO A SHOOT ON WEDNESDAY? YES, I THINK THAT'S ALL RIGHT. WHICH MODEL ARE YOU USING? YES, OK, I THINK I'LL ASK HER TO BRING HER BOOK ALONG BEFORE-HAND.

Later that morning he calls the agency .

H'MM . . . AMANDA, I'VE NOT MET HER BEFORE.

HELLO, JAMES HERE, I'M WORKING WITH AMANDA ON WEDNESDAY, IS THERE ANY CHANCE OF HER DROPPING IN WITH HER BOOK BEFORE THEN?

Amanda arrives with her book.

I SEE YOU'VE WORKED FOR PATCHES BEFORE, THEN?

Wednesday morning arrives, along with the Fashion Ed. and vast piles of clothes.

SO YOU WANT A WHITE BACKGROUND AND CROPPED SHOTS, I THINK WE CAN MANAGE THAT.

Leo, James's assistant starts to organise the lighting.

IF THEY'RE GOING TO CHANGE THEIR MINDS ABOUT THE LIGHTING, I HOPE THEY TELL ME BEFORE I'VE SET IT ALL UP.

While James puts the finishing touches to the lighting, and the Fashion Ed. checks Amanda's make-up and first outfit, the hardworking Leo helps out with a bit of ironing.

SIGH . . . AND I THOUGHT IT WAS GOING TO BE ALL LIMELIGHT AND GLAMOUR!

James checks the focus and lighting, then takes a Polaroid to make sure that everything is right before putting the shots on film.

James and Leo study the Polaroid, and, satisfied that everything's OK, James proceeds to take a couple of rolls of film.

During a break in the session, James nips up to the processing lab to check that the film is being processed the way he wants.

Next day . . . the finished article!

And everyone lives happily ever after!

Give your old clothes a brand new look!

OW many times have you looked in your wardrobe and thought: I've got nothing to wear — even though it's full to overflowing with all kinds of clothes? The trouble is, human nature being it is, you always get fed up of what you have got, hanker for what you haven't!

Even worse if one of your mates gets something new you come home to your old rags, feeling like old-Hand Rose.

Don't despair — you'd be amazed at how much can be done to bring your old stuff bang up to date again. All you'll need are scissors, needles and thread — and a dose of imagination.

Set out to prove to you that even the most dated clothes can be given a new lease of life with a little clever adjustin.

Rummaging round our cast-offs, we came up with the tacky collection of clothes you see in the first picture. There's an old shapeless T-shirt, a pair of baggy dungarees, a dirty pair of plimsolls, and to top the lot, fur coat of Gran's which was about to be consigned the dustbin.

the "after" picture, you can see how the outfit's been brought bang up to date again and is just as eye-catching as a brand new one! And the only new thing we bought were the braces. Read on to find out how it was done

DUNGAREES

the dungarees had a tear in them es braces fit on to the so they looked old, anyway, so we decided to do away bodice completely.

el to do fully unpick it from the band at the the trousers and join the seams of the waistband again (see pic.).

this, we straps off the the waistband, enough to mall hem and base the of in line front.

Inner hem edge, they very happy so we to make them a bit sewed up a 1.5 cm hem it, leaving a narrow and inserted I cm through here.

pulled in to make the tight at as, before the ends nettle were gether and the opening asting closed up.

Men's adjustable braces from C & A, £1.99.

THAT WAS THEN... THIS IS NOW!

OK, hands up all those who've ever dreamed of becoming a top fashion model? It's an ambition shared by loads of girls, but modelling's a very difficult business to break into and the competition's so intense that a dream is usually as far as it ever gets. Some girls do make it, of course — and Patches is happy to have played a small part in helping one girl to achieve her dream . . .

KIM ROBERTSON came in to do a photographic session for Patches when she was a shy sixteen year old. The picture on the left shows the way she looked then. We thought she had promise in those days — and we were right!

Kim is from Aberdeen and after her photograph appeared in Patches, a local model and promotions agency contacted her and asked if she would do some work for them.

This led to Kim taking part in fashion shows and all kinds of modelling from promoting retail products for supermarkets to glamourising a car at a motor show and earning a small fortune in a couple of hours at a race night organised by a big oil company.

After a few very successful months Kim did consider going south to London and joining one of the large agencies there as a full time model. But as she says:

"I'm a home town girl at heart. I work as a receptionist in a small hotel here and I enjoy that type of work. I like modelling as well, but it's a pretty insecure life. You never know if you'll be working from one day to the next."

So Kim decided to reject the glamour of London and stick to her Scottish roots.

Now, however, her part-time career has taken a surge forward. She was runner-up in the recent Miss Scotland finals. We asked Kim if she'd enjoyed being on the catwalk in front of hundreds of people . . .?

"I thought I'd be really nervous, but I wasn't too bad once I got there. The thing that did surprise me was all the back-stage bickering between the girls. I thought we'd all be nervous and that that would bring us together, but it was really a case of every girl for herself!"

Kim's prize as runner up included £800 cash, £300 worth of clothing vouchers, plus champagne and flowers. Had she won, she would have been guaranteed modelling jobs for her year's reign.

"I would have quite liked travelling around for a year, I think, although I'm sure I'd have been glad to get back to Scotland at the end of it all!" But she has just returned from the Miss International competition which was held in Tokyo. She wasn't a finalist, but she won a special prize — for being the girl with the best figure!

It was Kim's first time out of Scotland — she couldn't have gone much further away!

Though she didn't win, Kim says it's an experience she'll never forget.

Kim's favourite type of work is photographic modelling — but she enjoys fashion shows too, where she gets the chance to try on designer clothes. One of her latest jobs was promoting the 'Nessie Hunt' in Inverness — home of the famous Loch Ness Monster — a real case of Beauty and the Beast!

You can see from the recent photograph of Kim that the shy little girl has blossomed into a confident beauty. She doesn't know if she'll continue to enter beauty competitions but if she does, we wish her the best of luck and we're proud to say — we saw her first!

"But I wanted to be a BRAIN SURGEON..."

Going out and looking for a job is probably the most important thing you'll ever do, so it's important you go after the right one and don't end up doing something you hate. To give you a hand, we've spoken to six girls, just like you, about their jobs — how they found them, the good points and the bad points . . .

Tracy Adam (18) Trainee Insurance Broker

"I was almost seventeen when I left school with 8 O-levels and 4 A-levels. I went to college to study Secretarial Studies with French so I could become a bilingual secretary working abroad.

"I hated the course but I stuck it out to the end. I'm glad I did because it seems to be quite a good qualification — I was offered a few jobs but decided to take this one as a trainee insurance broker.

"I do some filing and typing but most of the time I'm phoning round insurance companies trying to get the best deal for a client. Any claims come through us too. I'm also on day release at a local college.

"I quite like the job but the money's pretty dreadful so I'd like to set up on my own one day.

"I like dealing with the public and using the phone and the hours are pretty good — nine to five, five days a week and an hour each day for lunch.

"People think insurance is boring — I don't but you have to be really interested in it to do well."

For information write to: The Careers Information Officer, The Chartered Insurance Institute, 20 Aldermanbury, London EC2V 7HY.

Samantha Smith (19) Hairdresser

"I had four 'O'-levels when I left school and I started working in an office. I'd been working in a hairdressers on Saturdays, so when I found out how much I hated office work and they offered me a full-time job, I took it like a shot!

"Training takes three years and then you spend two years as an improver. I'm in my fourth year just now and do everything from dry trims to perms and colour.

"There're lots of good things about this job — being able to talk all day, for a start! And it's great when someone comes in looking really horrible and they go home looking great.

"There are some bad points to the job too, though. I don't like people who come in for a dry trim and obviously haven't washed their hair for at least a week! And then there are the clients who demand a style I know won't suit them or is impossible to do with their type of hair.

"It's possible to train at a college but I think I've done the right thing training in a salon. Rather than learning from one or two teachers, there's a whole team of stylists to watch and learn from — all with their own style.

"I like this job a lot — I don't think I could do anything else now."

There are three ways to train as a hairdresser. Either at college full-time, or in a salon sometimes plus day-release at college or at a fee-paying private school like Vidal Sassoon (a very expensive way to learn!).

If you'd like to take up hairdressing, write to local salons and colleges and try to get some experience as a Saturday worker in a salon.

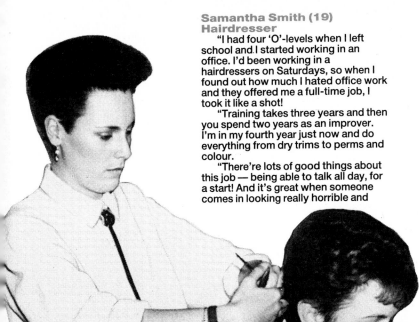

81

Sharon Soulsby (18) Sales Assistant

"I left school after 5th year with 8 O-levels and 1 A-level. At first I wanted to work in a travel agency but I ended up getting a job as a sales assistant in a boutique and decided I really liked it. Then after a while I changed jobs and came here, but it's much the same.

"I work 5 days a week and do a variety of jobs from handling the merchandise to being on the till. I enjoy it because you meet a lot of people and most of the time they're nice, but you do get awkward customers to deal with sometimes.

"This sort of work can be very tiring but after a while you get used to being on your feet all day. I prefer it when the shop's busy anyway. It's a real drag when things are quiet.

"One of the perks of the job is the discount I get on clothes. I get a third off anything I buy from here and that makes quite a saving.

"I'd say a job like this needs stamina — and patience when dealing with those difficult customers! You have to keep cheerful when you're serving too. And of course it helps to have a good eye for clothes and be interested in what you're selling.

"I'd like to stay in this business and hopefully get into the management side of things eventually . . ."

If you feel you'd enjoy a job like Sharon's, it's a good idea to find Saturday work as a sales assistant first. That way you'll discover if it really is what you want to do and if you do decide to look for a full-time position on leaving school, it'll be a good recommendation to a future employer.

Jill Wood (21) Riding Instructor

"Although you don't need masses of qualifications to train as a riding instructor (four 'O' levels) I stayed on at school to gain as many qualifications as I could.

"I got seven 'O' Grades and three Highers, so if I ever have to give up horses, I'll have something else to fall back on.

"The first instructors exam is the BHSAI — British Horse Society Assistant Instructor and I did mine as a working pupil, working in a yard in return for training.

"The next stage is the II — Intermediate Instructor, but I'd like to gain a lot more experience before I attempt that, so I feel confident of passing.

"So since gaining my AI, I've worked in a racing stud, a vet's, a tack shop, a dealer's yard and now I'm working in a private Mountain and Moorland stud/eventing yard, schooling eventers and eventing my own novice horse.

"Eventually, I'd like to go back to Scotland, where I come from, and set up my own livery yard, breaking and schooling young horses. And my ambition is to ride dressage for Britain!

"For anyone thinking of making horses their career, I'd say work hard at school to pass exams — you might be glad of them one day.

"Because so many young girls want to work with horses, there are lots of people willing to exploit you, so try to choose a BHS approved yard to train in and get a proper contract of employment.

"It's a great way of life if you're dedicated enough."

If you think this sounds like the life for you, try to get as much experience as you can before leaving school.

Write to local riding schools and livery yards for weekend work, and for career details, write to: The Careers Secretary, Training and Development Department, British Horse Society, National Equestrian Centre, Stoneleigh, Warwickshire, CV8 2LR.

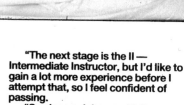

Karen Ramsay (21) Waitress

"I left school when I was sixteen. I didn't have any qualifications, but after an interview, I was accepted for technical college to do a City and Guilds certificate in General Catering.

"When I left, I was offered a job in the Victoria Hotel as holiday relief and then full-time. And I'm still here, nearly five years later!

"I love being a waitress, even though the hours are pretty long and I often have to work weekends. I suppose that's something you have to put up with though, because it's at weekends when people aren't working that they want to go out for meals!

"I like meeting all the different people — it's amazing what you can learn about someone who just comes in for a plate of spaghetti and ends up telling you their life story!

"We have lots of regulars I've come to know quite well too, and the only customers who're a bit annoying are the ones who choose a meal, then change their mind just as the chef finishes cooking it!

"Yep, you need to be pretty patient to be a waitress — and you need a strong pair of legs too!"

If you think your legs could stand it and you fancy working as a waitress, contact your local technical college for details of courses, or write to local hotels and restaurants.

Lorna Crawford (21) Veterinary Student

"I've wanted to be a vet since I was at primary school. I left school at eighteen with six Scottish Highers and came to the Royal Dick School of Veterinary Studies in Edinburgh. It takes five years to qualify and I'm in my third year just now.

"The course is hard work and even during the holidays we spend a lot of time doing work experience on farms and with vets.

"While I was still at school, I got in touch with a local vet and he agreed to take me out on his rounds with him to gain some experience. Eventually I went out every Wednesday afternoon and I learned a lot that way, so it's a good idea to do this if you're interested in a veterinary career.

"When I qualify, I'd like to work abroad for a while, probably in Australia or Canada and I'd like to work mainly with horses.

"To anyone who wants to be a vet I'd give this advice. Work really hard at school — you need good qualifications to get in to any of the six vet colleges in Britain. You'll have to work hard and be prepared to do some pretty unpleasant jobs — there's a lot more to it than cuddly kittens!

"The prospects are excellent — at the moment there aren't any unemployed vets in Britain and that's because the colleges only take a few people on the course each year. The Royal Dick take fifty-four, so there's a lot of competition for just a few places.

"I'm sure all the hard work will be worth it, though!"

To gain entry to a vet college, you'll need either three A-levels — an A in both Chemistry and Physics or Maths and a B in Biology or Zoology.

In Scotland, you'll need five Highers — three A's (preferably Chemistry, Physics and Biology) and two B's.

For careers information, write to the British Veterinary Association, 7 Mansfield Street, London W1M 0HT.

If Your Heart Isn't In It...

HEY, JOE — FANCY A GAME OF SQUASH TOMORROW MORNING? WE SHOULD BE ABLE TO BOOK A COURT IF WE GET TO THE SPORTS CENTRE EARLY ENOUGH.

YEAH, GREAT. YOU'LL SLAUGHTER ME, THOUGH — I'M NOT UP TO YOUR STANDARD.

I REALLY FANCY PAUL. I WISH I COULD GET TO KNOW HIM BETTER — BUT HE ONLY SEEMS TO BE INTERESTED IN SPORT AND I'M HOPELESS AT GAMES.

WE HAVEN'T GOT ANYTHING IN COMMON, AND I CAN'T JUST GO UP TO HIM AND START TALKING, I DON'T HAVE THE NERVE.

I WOULDN'T BE HIS TYPE, ANYWAY. A GIRL'D NEED TO BE REALLY FIT AND ATHLETIC TO CATCH HIS EYE ...

IT'S FUNNY — HE OUGHT TO BE REALLY BORING, THE WAY HE'S SO OBSESSED WITH SPORT. BUT HE ISN'T, EVERYONE SAYS HE'S DEAD NICE WHEN YOU GET TO KNOW HIM. I JUST WISH I WAS MORE SPORTY ...

Then . . .

WHAT'S THAT, MARIE?

PAUL'S LATEST IDEA TO RAISE MONEY FOR THE CLUB. HE'S ORGANISING A FUN RUN NEXT MONTH.

IT'S NOT MY IDEA OF FUN, GOING FOR A SIX-MILE RUN AND PAYING FOR THE PRIVILEGE. BUT I GUESS SOME SUCKERS'LL FALL FOR IT!

IT'S NOT MY IDEA OF FUN, EITHER — BUT IT'D BE A GREAT WAY OF GETTING PAUL'S ATTENTION, IF I WENT IN FOR IT! THAT'D MAKE HIM NOTICE ME, IF ANYTHING DID ...

So I wrote my name on the list, right under Paul's . . .

AFTER ALL, YOU DON'T HAVE TO BE SUPER-FIT TO RUN SIX MILES. LOTS OF ORDINARY PEOPLE DO IT, SO WHY CAN'T I?

My friends thought I was mad . . .

But I knew it'd be worth it . . .

So . . .

Next morning . . .

But, before I'd gone a hundred yards . . .

Continued on page 88

BACK*CHAT*

Unless your head can turn 180°, it's unlikely that you have much idea of how you look from behind. Maybe you don't think it's very important, but here're a couple of situations where your back view may give more away about you than you'd like.

You're all dolled up for a party when you clap eyes on the school's answer to Nick Kamen, then you sidle up and brush past him. He turns to see who that Vision of Loveliness could be, only to be faced with a pair of tatty stilettos, squint stockings, droopy underskirt, and a hairdo that looks like it needs a rake and hedgeclippers to sort it out. The same thing can happen after you've waved goodbye at your first job interview.

Not a very attractive image, is it? So here are a few tips on how to avoid having a monster behind you . . .

PAT YOURSELF ON THE BACK . . . if you make good use of the loofah to keep your back as clean as your face. Discourage spots by keeping long hair away from your skin.

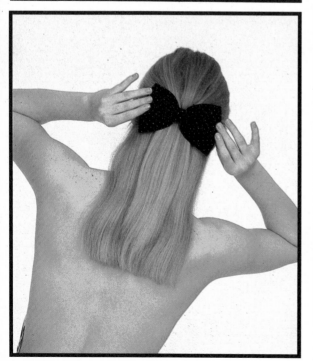

HAIRPIECES Whether short or long, hair should at least be brushed and trimmed regularly. Spare a few moments away from brushing your eyebrows to tame that mane.

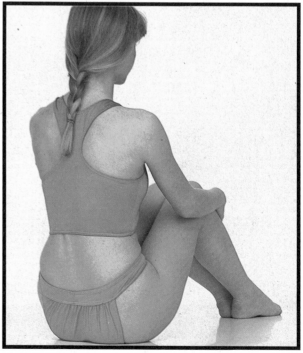

THE BOTTOM LINE Good posture holds all your blobby bits in place, makes you look slimmer and lets your muscles work properly. If you intend to take to the beach in a thongy thing this summer, better start the bottom walking now. The loofah will come in handy too, to slough off pimply thighs and get your circulation going.

LEGGING IT Legs tend to dry up, having less oil glands than the rest of your body, so spare a bit of moisturiser for them. If they're shapeless, cycling exercises or swimming should tone them up. Check your tights for ladders — splintery school chairs can catch you out, so if your pins aren't whiter than white, it may be cheaper to opt for ankle socks.

FOOTNOTES Shoes that are sparkling at the front shouldn't have chipped tatty heels, especially as there are heel-paints available to cover up the damage. Shoe bows and fancy tights can transform tired old plates of meat into dancing feet. Keep the high heels for special occasions and you won't have to look forward to a future of twisted ankles and bulging bunions. (That's what my gran says, anyway.)

They wouldn't leave me alone . . .

LOOK, JUST GO HOME, WILL YOU?

NO, WE WANT TO COME TOO!

I KNOW, SALLY, WE'LL HAVE A RACE! HE CAN BE SEB COE, AND I'M STEVE CRAM, RIGHT?

In the end, I just gave up and went home . . .

I MIGHT'VE KNOWN IT WASN'T SAFE TO GO OUT ROUND HERE WHERE EVERYONE KNOWS ME. SOME LOUDMOUTH WAS BOUND TO SPOT ME — AND I HATE BEING LAUGHED AT!

I began wearing my tracksuit down to the club, and . . .

HI, SAL! BEEN TRAINING? GOOD GIRL! COME ON, I'LL BUY YOU A COKE.

IT'S WORKING! PAUL'S BEEN REALLY FRIENDLY RECENTLY. AND IT'LL BE EVEN BETTER AFTER THE FUN RUN, HE'LL REALLY RESPECT ME THEN . . .

THERE'S NO NEED TO TRAIN OUTSIDE, REALLY — JOGGING ON THE SPOT'S JUST AS GOOD! I RECKON IF I DO HALF AN HOUR A DAY, I'LL SOON BE FIT . . .

When the day finally came . . .

I CAN'T SEE PAUL ANYWHERE! I NEVER THOUGHT THERE'D BE AS MANY PEOPLE AS THIS RUNNING. STILL, HE'S BOUND TO BE UP NEAR THE FRONT SOMEWHERE . . .

I elbowed my way to the front, just as the run started . . .

I STILL CAN'T SEE HIM — BUT NEVER MIND. HE'LL WORK HIS WAY THROUGH THE PACK SOON, AND HE'LL BE REALLY IMPRESSED, FINDING ME UP IN THE LEAD LIKE THIS . . .

But ten minutes later there was still no sign of him — and I had other problems . . .

THIS IS HARDER WORK THAN JOGGING IN THE BEDROOM EVER WAS! I'M OUT OF BREATH ALREADY — AND I'VE GOT A STITCH COMING ON, I CAN FEEL IT . . .

I struggled on — but soon . . .

THIS STITCH IS KILLING ME, I CAN'T BREATHE AND I FEEL SICK . . . IT'S NO GOOD, I'VE HAD IT! I WAS A FOOL TO THINK IT'D BE SO EASY . . .

And finally . . .

So that's what we did — but . . .

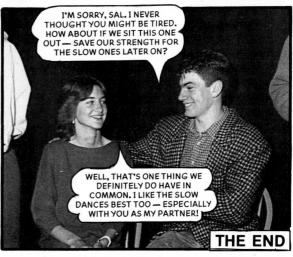

THE END

PATCHES Morten

BEAT THE

BOY BLUES

It's happened, the impossible. He's packed you in and all you want to do is rage and cry at the same time. You're in a bad way and your mind's playing funny tricks on you and, no matter how hard you try, you can't seem to think of a single bad point about him, he's suddenly been transformed into an angel and it upsets you even more to think this divine creature has just walked out of your life.

This is grade one misery. True blue despair. The pits. You're sopping around all day, playing those same old records over and over again. You've lost interest in everything, even food!

There's no point in anyone trying to tell you any different, you *know* you'll never meet anyone else and you'll never smile again — EVER!

But although it doesn't seem like it right now there are ways of coming to terms with what you see as the worst tragedy of your life.

If you find yourself thinking about him all the time, don't fight it but try instead to concentrate on his bad points — if he hasn't got any, invent them! What about the time he turned up late for the party, spent most of the evening dancing with your best friend and then had the cheek to ask *you* why you were so quiet!

Or what about that time you were lovingly wrapped in a romantic cuddle, he got a faraway look in his eyes, you thought he was about to whisper something sloppy, you held your breath, looked up into his eyes and he said, "Just think, if Liverpool win their next away match they'll be top of the league"!

When you think about it really hard, having a boyfriend is all very nice but it can be a bit of a bind too. You don't have as much time to go out and have a laugh with your mates. You worry constantly about putting on weight and getting spots in case he goes off you.

When you go out for a meal you feel that you've got to keep up a ladylike image and delicately nibble at your food whereas normally you'd scoff the lot in five minutes. You have to pretend to be interested when he and his friends conduct endless boring conversations about the latest in motorbikes.

You can't eye up the local talent in the same way in case it gets back to him and he goes all moody. Then, without even realising it, you suddenly find yourself standing in the freezing cold at the local football pitch watching him play footie. And if all that's not bad enough you have to be a complete mug and give away your last Rolo!

Is he really worth the heartache?

SCHOOL BLUES

You think it's the end of your school career. You've just failed all your exams, you're fighting hard to control the tears, you can picture your mum shaking her head disappointedly and you're too scared to even think about telling your dad. You're now officially branded a dumbo and there seems to be no point in picking up your pen ever again.

But is it really that bad? The main thing to remember is that if you're determined enough it's only a temporary setback. With a lot of hard work you'll be able to make up those extra marks to finally drag yourself over the pass line.

There are very few natural brainboxes in the world and even Einstein's bound to have failed an exam! That swotty looking girl who sits at the front of the class with her finger constantly hovering over her high tec. digital calculator isn't really brigher than you, it's just that she puts in more man hours.

First step in your sure-fire plan to boost your IQ is to get organised. Develop a system where you can keep track of what you've got to do when — and do it! Each time you learn a new topic, summarise the main points in one notebook and you'll find revision for exams much easier because the bulk of the information is in the one place. You'll also eliminate the problem of searching frantically at midnight through a mountain of paperwork to find that one crucial piece of paper that's got your only copy of a vital chemistry formula scrawled on it.

Getting round to attacking your homework is always a major problem but when you find that you'd even sit and watch "Songs of Praise" rather than open your books, you know you're in a bad way. Try to tackle the most difficult stuff first — leaving it in your bag all night won't make it any easier and the answers won't magically come to you while you're eating your Sugar Puffs next morning.

At least if you start your homework early enough you have a chance to ask someone, preferably your teacher, for help. The other point to remember is that if you're stuck with some obscure mathematical formula that sends huge waves of nausea over you just looking at it, never mind understanding it, you can always actually ask your teacher to explain it — not nearly so gruesome as you imagine and it is actually what he's there for.

When you get your homework back, don't sneak a look at your mark and throw your jotter away in disgust. Sit down and go through it all calmly and make a note of everything that was marked wrong, try to work out where you made your mistake and learn from it.

If you don't understand your error — ask!

DIET BLUES

It's no good, you see it, think about it, dream about it all the time, you're becoming obsessed, life has no meaning unless there are plates of steaming hot, tasty nosh hovering just in front of you . . . All these symptoms are signs that you've finally reached breaking point in your battle with the sweet jar.

There seems to be nothing you can do to stop the slide and you're well on the way to the big blow out. Chips, chocolate and ice-cream a-plenty are about to be devoured by your slavering chops.

So what do you do? Give up for good and resign yourself to being forever a fatty? No, there is a way to let the slim tantalising creature inside you loose upon the world. What you have to do is stop thinking about it.

Relax. Don't think in terms of being "on a diet". Try to work towards a sensible attitude to food, making sure you eat a wide variety of fruit, vegetables, carbohydrates, protein, fibre and avoid salts, sugars and fats wherever possible. Even if you do have the odd gorging session just try to look on it as a temporary setback and don't think, "Oh, well, I've broken my diet now, I may as well stuff my face for the next week."

Although counting calories is a good way to keep a rough guide on how much you're scoffing, don't become obsessed by it. It'll look pretty strange if at lunchtime you whip out a set of kitchen scales to weigh your diet-sized portion of coleslaw.

Just settle for keeping a rough

BLUES!

tally of your calorie intake but don't panic if you have a large apple instead of a medium-sized one. Remember too that you can allow yourself the odd treat as long as that means treating yourself to one biscuit rather than one packet!

The old idea of sticking a picture of a glamorous model on the side of the fridge is really just a waste of time. When the food fever hits, you become remarkably good at averting your eyes. Far better to pin up a picture of Christopher Biggins and console yourself with the happy knowledge that you're nowhere near that chubby.

As you gradually learn to stop worrying about food, you'll find that you eat a much more balanced diet that includes a wide variety of food and is healthier for you. By that time you'll be so relaxed about what you eat that even if you scoff three Mars Bars in a row, you'll enjoy them!

TRUE BLUES

Even if you're not bothered by any of these particular problems you could still find that you're getting fed-up about nothing in particular. But no matter how bad things seem there are always a few steps you can take to put an end to your misery.

One of the best ways to lift a bad mood is to get a change of scene. Even if you just go out for a walk it'll help to clear your head. Always try to find a sympathetic person to discuss your worries with. Even if that person can't give you any answers, simply talking about things helps you to work out just exactly what the problem is.

You could try reading the problem pages of as many magazines as you can get your hands on — you're bound to find someone who's in a worse position than you are!

Thinking of others is always a good way of keeping your own problems in perspective. If there are any elderly people who live near you, go out and pay them a visit rather than sitting in moping.

Alternatively, try picking up the phone and calling some of your friends. You never know, one of them could be feeling down too .

Whatever you decide to do, don't just sit around feeling miserable. Your problem won't go away by itself and you'll probably feel a lot better just knowing you're trying to do something about it.

Continued from page 3

Bearing all this in mind, Porky gave Hal a call . . .

SO THAT'S SETTLED THEN? YOU'RE COMING UP FOR A FEW DAYS?

YOU BETCHA! I WOULDN'T MISS THE CHANCE TO SPEND TIME WITH YOUR PIGS!

I MUST SAY I'M IMPRESSED WITH HOW WELL THESE PIGLETS ARE LOOKING. BUT PIGS ASIDE, YOUNG PETER, WHAT IS THERE FOR A CHAP TO DO IN THE EVENINGS ROUND HERE?

WELL, SINCE YOU MENTION IT, THE BIG FARM UP THE ROAD IS HAVING BARN DANCES EVERY SATURDAY NIGHT ALL THROUGH THE SUMMER. YOU COULD GO ALONG TONIGHT.

Porky and Hal went out in the car to find the farm so that Hal would know where to go at night. And on the way back . . .

TAKE A LOOK AT HER, PETER. SHE'S A BIT DIFFERENT FROM THE LOCAL TALENT, ISN'T SHE?

YES, THAT'S CHARLOTTE. SHE'S JUST ABOUT SUITABLE FOR YOU, HAL. VERY RICH. CLASSY.

Later that night . . .

WELL, I'M OFF THEN. WISH ME LUCK.

HAVE FUN. IF YOU HIT IT OFF WITH CHARLOTTE, BY ALL MEANS BRING HER BACK FOR A COFFEE OR SOMETHING . . .

As Porky expected, Hal and Charlotte got on like a haystack on fire . . .

I'M SO GLAD TO HAVE MET YOU, HAL. YOU HAVE SO MUCH MORE CLASS THAN THE LOCALS.

WHY DON'T WE LEAVE NOW, CHARLOTTE. THE NIGHT IS STILL YOUNG . . .

It was a warm summer evening . . .

WE CAN GO BACK TO MY COUSIN'S FOR A COFFEE, AND THEN WE CAN TAKE A ROMANTIC STROLL . . .

OH, THAT SOUNDS JUST LOVELY.

Porky had known that sooner or later, Hal's conversation would turn to pigs . . .

WELL, TO BE PERFECTLY HONEST, I'M NOT REALLY A GREAT PIG FAN . . .

94